A Fa

W

Beli

A Faith
Worth
Believing

Finding New Life Beyond the Rules of Religion

TOM STELLA

HarperSanFrancisco
A Division of HarperCollinsPublishers

FIRST EDITION
Library of Congress Cataloging-in-Publication Data
is available upon request.

ISBN 0–06–056343–5

04 05 06 07 08 RRD(H) 10 9 8 7 6 5 4 3 2 1

My Christianity has become compost . . . [a] pile of organic substance transforming into a ground, a matrix into which we must mix other elements for the next seeds to sprout. . . . If our traditions and symbols are truly part of living, then they are organic and will have rhythms of living and dying.

EMILY CULPEPPER

Perhaps the greatest disaster of human history is one that happened to or within religion: that is the conceptual division between the holy and the world, the excerpting of the Creator from creation.

WENDELL BERRY

The contemporary impression of myth as falsehood has . . . led people to think of them as fantasies passing as truth. But mythology is a vessel of the truth. . . . The spiritual needs of people are neglected by religious leaders who insist on reasserting the historical-factual character of religious metaphors.

JOSEPH CAMPBELL

This book is dedicated to my father, Andrew Stella, who through hard work, a sense of humor, a healthy disregard for decorum, and a love of life both embodied and pointed to the passionate reality that is the sacred wonder of our existence on this planet.

Contents

Acknowledgments

Gratitude and happiness, I have discovered, are compatible partners in the dance of life. I am grateful for the assistance of those whose names follow, for they have made this book come to life. And I am happy about knowing those among them who have not only made my writing better, but my life brighter.

Some members of my family have been instrumental in bringing this book to completion. First among them is my mother, Pearl, from whom I have inherited a sense for life's fragile but enduring sacredness. My brothers and sisters-in-law Bob and Joanne, and Mike and Pat, my sister, Beverly, and my nephew Jeffery have been personally supportive and generous with their computer savvy.

My friends Roger Cormier, Ray DeFabio, Dan Flora, and the Hosmers (Rosco, Joan, Kristin, Katie, Brian) have supported me along the way, and have offered helpful advice, needed encouragement, and constant affirmation.

I am indebted to the staff of the Tri-parish Community in Colorado Springs for their patience with my ineptness at the keyboard, most notably John Lendzion, Julie Pilant, and Alessandra Sentman. If you were frustrated with me, you hid it well.

This book would not have been published by Harper-SanFrancisco had it not been for Brennan Manning. His appreciation for my first book, and his persistent advocacy on my behalf convinced the folks at Harper to take a chance on me.

Finally, I am grateful for, and happy about my association with the very personal and professional people who work at HarperSanFrancisco who have had a hand in the making and marketing of this book: Margery Buchanan, Cindy DiTiberio, Roger Freet, Chris Hafner, Terri Leonard, Mickey Maudlin, Kathy Reigstad, and Jim Warner.

In a special way, I thank my editor, Julia Roller, who worked almost as hard on this book as I did. She is skilled at the delicate art of affirmation/challenge, and was able to make me feel good about what I had written at the same time that she "took it apart!" Her literary expertise and theological acumen made her invaluable in the editing process.

Introduction

I do not remember at what age I first became conscious of God, church, and religion, but I do recall that that awareness, when it developed, centered around feelings of fear and guilt. I had a haunting sense that God was displeased with me, and that I must find a way to become better than I was if I wanted to avoid an eternity in hell.

That way involved keeping the rules of religion—believing what my faith-tradition professed to be true, worshiping when and where it dictated, and acting in accord with its code of conduct. This was the ticket, the means by which I could enter the arena of God's embrace. I became intent on getting it right—that is, on pleasing/appeasing God—and I became discontent with myself when I failed to do so.

The belief system by which I was nurtured also instilled in me a sensitivity to the passing nature of life as we know it, and a belief in the primacy of an infinite reality yet to be realized. I learned that the world was both a temporary place and a place of temptation, a proving ground that, if negotiated well, led to an eternity of bliss in heaven.

In conversation with people from a variety of faith-traditions, I have found that my earliest religious recollections and associations are similar to theirs. Independent of the particulars unique to each religion, there are elements of a common belief having to do with God's being less than happy with humanity, with obedience to religious dictates being the means of assuaging this divine dissatisfaction, and with the world being the place where we earn the right to spend eternity with God.

Many people live their lives content with the interpretation of religious truths they learned in their childhood. Some of them cling tightly to their beliefs and judge harshly anyone who does not. A greater number, motivated by traditional understandings of the topics we will consider in these chapters, live positive, productive, and caring lives. But others of us, for a variety of reasons, reach a point when what once made sense in the realm of religion does so no longer. It is at this juncture that we are invited to recognize that there is a deeper meaning to the teachings and truths traditional religion espouses, and a more profound dimension to ourselves than we had ever imagined.

I grew up believing the teachings of the Catholic Church practically without question until I was in college. At that time the study of existential philosophy brought me to the realization that my beliefs had been a crutch upon which I leaned to get through life, to answer unanswerable questions, to deny the apparent randomness and absurdity of the human condition. This was truly a time of crisis. The solid foundation upon which my life had rested, the matrix of meaning that had formed the infrastructure of my self-understanding, the sense of security that had shielded me from life's harsher realities, crumbled in what seemed like an instant. How could I have believed for so long what now seemed to be without substance? How could I remain identified with a religious institution when its teachings and practices had ceased to have meaning? I didn't know then what I know now—namely, that doubt is an important phase in the process of faith-development and not necessarily an indication of faith's demise.

Over time, with an integrity that felt right to both head and heart, I was able to affirm the reality of God without having to deny the random reality of life in the world. I began to accept God as a companion in the chaos rather than someone who was sleeping on the job when bad things happened to good people. My childhood understanding of Jesus as one sent from on high to atone for our sins also began to change at this time, and I recognized and affirmed the holiness of his humanity more than I had previously.

As the shaken foundation of my faith began to settle, I was able to shift my focus from myself to the events that were unfolding in the world around me. I began graduate studies in theology in Washington, D.C., in 1967. Civil rights issues and the war in Vietnam were front-burner and front-page phenomena. Churches, my own and others, were becoming more aware of, and outspoken about, social issues, and the gospel was being viewed as a call to action rather than a handbook for personal piety or mandated morality.

This was a vital, if tumultuous, time in our nation's history. I breathed the air of this tumult in the city that was at the center of policymaking and the site of demonstrations objecting to those policies. Washington, D.C., was also a city, like many others that spring, that was ravaged by riots in response to the assassination of Martin Luther King Jr. My exposure to this atmosphere changed forever and for the better my understanding of the prophetic nature of religion and of the gospel, both of which call us to be fully *in* the world at the same time that they challenge us not to be *of* it.

Two experiences helped me to recognize that a person need not be separated from life in the world in order to be in touch with God—a false concept that had subtly taken root in me while I was ensconced in the seminary. Following the completion of graduate theological studies, I spent a year and a half acquiring a master's degree in counseling at the University of Michigan. Living on my own in a secular environment opened me to the realization that the values I had internalized from my faith-tradition were similar to those espoused by many non-Catholics, non-Christians, and nonbelievers. I met and found a soul-connection with people very different from me, religiously speaking, but very much one with me spiritually.

About six years later, and after functioning as a priest for five of those years, I began a leave of absence (during which I lived in Chicago and San Francisco) in order to rethink my commitment. The necessity of supporting myself financially thrust me into a world that was alien to me. Instead of being free to contemplate eternal truths and minister to those in need, I was having to think about everyday matters and attend to my own needs—to do what most people must do in order to survive and to support themselves and their families. As a result of this experience, I became less critical and more compassionate toward those who spend their time and energy on "worldly affairs." I became more aware of the sacredness of everyday life and of the need to discover in the workplace, at play, and in relationships the presence of the Holy that I had mistakenly believed was primarily in less earthy venues.

Exposure to contemplative spirituality has been a major factor in the way I view life and religion. Reading the works of Thomas Merton and being immersed periodically in a monastic environment have opened my eyes to a new way of seeing—one that recognizes the communion of humanity and Divinity. The realization of this truth pulled the rug out from under my traditional understanding of the function of religion. I no longer believe that I must, by adhering to the rules of religion, strive to win God's favor. Rather, I must learn to be attuned to God present within all creation. Contemplative spirituality has taught me that growth in God is primarily a matter of waking up to the mystery of life's holiness and living it with lighthearted reverence, passion, and compassion.

The study of scripture has been another influence in the development of my faith. Acknowledging the importance of a critical rather than a literal approach to scripture has enabled me to recognize the mythic nature of the truths that scripture expresses. I realize that the Bible is not historically/factually accurate in all, or even most, of what it relates, and that because this is so, its contents speak more powerfully to the realities of my life. No one writes more convincingly of this than comparative mythologist Joseph Campbell:

> Many elements of the Bible seem lifeless and unbelievable because they have been regarded as historical facts instead of metaphorical representations of spiritual realities.[1]
>
> Our religions have stressed too strongly the strictly historical aspect so that we are . . . in worship of the historical event, instead of being able to read through that event to the spiritual message.[2]

As I became open to the deeper meaning that emerges when we accept scripture's mythic/symbolic nature, I began to rethink my understanding of Jesus. I now see him not only as an historical person who was for some Jews of his time, and for Christians ever after, the fulfillment of Yahweh's promise, the long-awaited Messiah, but as an archetype, the one in whom is revealed the sacred self that is every person. This realization does not lessen Jesus' significance; on the contrary, it enables me to embrace the full, explosive meaning of his person and mine.

Another catalyst in my religious development was the study of traditions that are not Christian. Hinduism, Islam, Buddhism, Taoism, and Judaism, among others, are rich in wisdom and rooted in an understanding of life and of people that affirms our holiness. Despite the differences that abound within and between these and other belief systems, including Christianity, there is common ground and a basic sameness that has made it impossible for me to affirm that any one of them has a corner on the truth, but easy to proclaim that each has some elements of it.

This book is written for those who, like me, can no longer hold as literally true the religious stories and teachings that in the past may have gone unquestioned.

I have come to realize that my rootedness in traditional religious beliefs has left me rootbound and in need of room to grow. I have come to recognize that the farsightedness that focuses on what lies beyond has blurred my vision of the sacredness of the present and the presence of the Sacred here and now. I have come to embrace my need to move beyond belief to a faith worth believing, one that embraces this world, this life, and all humanity as holy ground.

When one awakens to the realization that he or she has outgrown the traditional interpretation of long-held beliefs, there is a tendency to throw out the baby with the bathwater, to turn away from anything having to do with religion.

Although many (perhaps most) people react in this fashion, at least for a time, others respond to this "crisis" as an opportunity to delve beneath the surface of their beliefs.

Because all truths are capable of being more fully understood, this approach often issues in the exciting discovery that beneath literal language lies mythic meaning. Joseph Campbell speaks to this truth when he states that "the connotations of religious metaphor are rich, timeless, and refer not to somebody else in the outer world of another era but to us and our inner spiritual experience right now."[3] In other words, there is another way to interpret the stories in scripture and a deeper significance to the truths expressed in creedal statements and liturgical language.

I regret that some readers may find my thoughts on these matters disturbing, or experience them as a threat to the system of beliefs that has given meaning to their lives. But I have come to a point in my life when I must state forcefully what I believe, and when I must either reject or redefine what I was taught about God, religion, church, and so on. I need to separate the truth from the tone, to keep the baby while I throw out the bathwater of my religious training—those elements, both formal and informal, that have ceased to make sense to my mind or engage my heart. The notion that God is a separate and distant entity and that I, through adherence to the teachings and practices of my faith-tradition, must earn the right to be with God when my life is over seems far from the truth Jesus embodied, and close to the teachings he spoke against.

The chapters that follow each begin with two quotations. The first, in every instance, is from *A Catechism of Christian Doctrine*. Although the content of that book is particularly Catholic (the tradition in which I was raised), I believe that anyone schooled in a mainline Christian denomination will recognize in it many elements of their belief system. In the first part of each chapter I articulate my understanding of the topic as I learned it in my early religious training. There is much to commend in what I was taught through the church and by others who were instrumental in forming my concepts in matters of faith. However, those truths were often communicated in a manner that was less than enlivening. They came with a "believe it or burn," "do it or die" undertone, leaving the impression that God was keeping score and that the fires of hell were a distinct possibility.

The second quote in each chapter, taken from a variety of sources, offers a deeper meaning to the subject under consideration. Reflecting that transition away from the literal, in the latter part of each chapter I present my understanding of the topic as I now embrace it. In every instance these new meanings have arisen from a need to satisfy an ultimate longing and a sense of belonging to something far more vast and intimate than was communicated through traditional teachings. What I have come to believe is based not on blind faith (the unquestioned acceptance of religious truths), but on *fides quarens intellectum* (faith seeking understanding), the desire to align what my soul senses to be true with what my mind can affirm. These new understandings are more catholic (universal) than they are Catholic. They are less stereotypically spiritual (removed from ordinary life) and more soulful (anchored in nature and human nature). They reflect an incarnational theology—one that affirms the sacredness of life, the truth of God's indwelling presence. They are my response to the clarion call of the Sacred arising from the heart of humanity, the core of creation.

Last, in each chapter I present some thoughts that flow from the way I now see and relate to the truths being considered. These meditations will, I hope, be thought-provoking. But I also hope that you will resonate with them at a deeper level; that they will connect with your own inner longing for belonging, and that they will serve to heighten a heartfelt awareness of your oneness with the sacred soul of life, the mystery we call God.

My intent in offering the reflections that conclude each chapter is that you will linger with them prayerfully. When we move beyond belief, we enter into the realm of faith. Here we are not involved in argumentation about religious/ theological teachings, but we are in a personal relationship with the subject of those teachings. I sincerely hope that my attempt to articulate the personal and intimate nature of this relationship will be a catalyst that invites you to both rest and revel in its reality. After the final meditation in each chapter, space is provided to write any thoughts, intuitions, feelings, etc, that may have occured to you while reflecting on these words.

I conclude this introduction by quoting an anonymous author who, I believe, had in mind the audience I wish to address when he wrote:

> There are some presently engaged in the active life who are being prepared by grace to grasp the message of this book. I am thinking of those who feel the mysterious action of the Spirit in their inmost being stirring them to love. I do not say that they continually feel this stirring, as experienced contemplatives do, but now and again they taste something of contemplative love in the very core of their being. Should

such folk read this book, I believe they will be greatly encouraged and reassured.[4]

It is my deepest hope that this book will challenge beliefs that may be limiting, and that it will bring you both encouragement and reassurance as you seek to respond to the stirrings of the Spirit that invite you to a faith worth believing.

COLORADO SPRINGS, COLORADO

Chapter 1

Religion

How can we prove that all men are obliged to practice religion? We can prove that all men are obliged to practice religion because all men are entirely dependent on God and must recognize that dependence by honoring Him and praying to Him.

A CATECHISM OF CHRISTIAN DOCTRINE

Religion responds to a wide variety of human needs: needs for belonging, for security, for moral responsibility, and for belonging to community, as well as more clearly spiritual needs for experiencing the mystery and meaning of being.

GERALD MAY,
WILL AND SPIRIT

As I learned it in my youth, there were only two kinds of people in the world: those who believed in God and those who did not, those who went to church and those who stayed home, those who had religion and those who were going to hell.

Religion, consisting of creed (teachings), cult (worship), and code (law), was a fixed and solid system that anchored me in an ancient tradition. Its teachings and expectations were clearly defined and, if I kept its rules and embraced its dictates, I was assured of an eternal reward, a place in heaven. The era in which I learned about religion taught me that it was primarily a private affair, not a prophetic one, a vertical matter having to do with the state of my soul before God. I had only to believe what I was taught, worship when it was prescribed, and keep my own house clean—my soul free from sin—in order to rest secure in the knowledge that God was pleased with me.

Religion was also parochial—a sort of holy nationalism that espoused an "us against them" mentality. In the past, this attitude gave birth to atrocities such as the Crusades, religious wars that sanctioned slaughtering the infidel. In the present, it is the underlying cause of many of the world's conflicts—conflicts that are, according to psychologist Eugene Kennedy, "the bitter harvest of the distortions of religious teachings planted long ago."[1] An obvious "bitter harvest" raging in our own time, one fueled by the events of September 11, 2001, is a renewal of conflict and misunderstanding between Muslims and Christians. Fundamentalists on both sides are quick to quote their scriptures in an attempt to vilify one another and support their own violent attitudes and actions.

Parochialism has also fueled a missionary mindset that has sent some to foreign lands to convert pagans and others to front doors across the nation to convince believers that they aren't believing the right things. I grew up breathing the parochial air that told me Catholics not only had a corner on the truth, but *the* corner on *the* truth. I don't remember whether it was actually considered a sin, but Catholics were instructed not to enter any Protestant church or Jewish synagogue—not even to attend a wedding or funeral. This made me wonder whether there was such a thing as religious cooties!

When I was growing up, you were considered a religious person if you were baptized and if you "practiced." Most of the people I knew practiced once a week; that is, they attended church on Sundays and put money in the basket that was passed among the people. This kind of practice meant that you were a solid citizen, an upstanding person. It meant that you weren't likely to harm your neighbor, though you might be known to get into an altercation after church in an attempt to be the first one out of the parking lot.

But there was another kind of religious person, the kind who wasn't afraid to say the word *God* out loud, who quoted from the Bible, and who knew that he or she was saved and that you were not. These people were "born again"; they were on fire with the Holy Spirit. I was a pretty religious kid when I was growing up, but "born agains" made my devotion seem inadequate. I was self-conscious about believing in God and private about the practice of religion. I wasn't proud to be a Catholic or a Christian; I was just too afraid of God *not* to be. I experienced religious people of this ilk as self-righteous (narrow-minded and judgmental) and overzealous; we used to call them "holy rollers" because their enthusiasm for God seemed to take them over emotionally when they worshiped. I preferred to be in the company of rock-and-rollers!

The religion of my youth was a great comfort on one hand, and a terrible burden on the other. There was a security in knowing what it took to be on the "straight and narrow," and in knowing that, if I strayed, the way back was clearly marked—the well-trod path of repentance and confession. And there was a comforting warmth that came from wrapping myself in the routine rituals that religion provided. They were like a cocoon, though I wonder now how much metamorphosis was taking place.

The burden of religion was the awful realization that, try as I might, I could not stay on the right path. No resolve of mine (regardless how sincere), and no amount of willpower (no matter how strong), was ever able to sustain my good intentions. Though there was no need to fear God's wrath if I lived well, there was nonetheless always reason to fear, since I never lived well for very long. Hypervigilance, low-grade guilt, and bouts of scrupulosity were a common outcome of the failure and fear that accompanied this brand of religion. The end result was that religion became a cause for dejection rather than a source of joy, a means of manipulating God instead of a vehicle through which I could relate to and celebrate the reality of the ongoing mercy and love that is God. Episcopal priest and theologian Robert Farrar Capon states it this way:

> Since we always fail somewhere, our attitude toward the all-important something turns out to be . . . one of apprehension, if not downright fear—a state of perpetual jitters at being charged with malpractice over some item of creed, cult, or conduct. Religion commonly professes to love the something it's trying to establish a relationship with, but in fact its program is aimed less at love than at such things as appeasement, propitiation, self-protection, conjuring, and control.[2]

As with so many others in my generation, the brand of religion I internalized was a matter of requirements that presumed God was *against* rather than *for* me; it created a sense of self that hovered close to the minimum standard for acceptability. In life as well as in school, flunking religion was always a distinct possibility.

Despite the negative and misleading notions implanted by my early religious training, it provided me with some important concepts that have enabled me to relate to what I cannot see but which I experience within—a primal intuition of God. William Wordsworth gives expression to this state of innocent oneness and to the inevitability of its disappearance in his poem "Intimations of Immortality":

> There was a time when meadow, grove, and stream,
> The earth, and every common sight,
> To me did seem
> Appareled in celestial light,
> The glory and the freshness of a dream.
> It is not now as it hath been of yore;—
> Turn whereso'er I may,
> By night or day,
> The things which I have seen I see no more.[3]

The role of religion is to reconnect us to the awareness that we are one with the Mystery, the ray of "celestial light." The images and stories that institutional religion uses to do this are limited and colored by the experiences of those who communicate them, but without them I would have been at a loss to name the archetypal reality that my intuition presented to me. Perhaps buying into those stories literally was a necessary phase, like crawling before walking, but it is embarrassing to realize how long I was content with them. I know now that I value the function of religion more than ever, but my soul longs for an understanding of it that is less rigid and more expansive.

There are not, I now realize, two kinds of people in the world; we are all one body. There is no wrathful God in a place called heaven, but one vast Mystery in whose life we share. There is a private dimension to our relationship with God, but in God we are rooted in the world and intimately united with all humanity. I need religion in order to remain aware of the deepest truths of life, and to help me walk to the rhythm of a different (and divine) drummer, one who invites me to be "in the world, but not of it."

There is a story about a man who learned that a wise spiritual master was living close by. In his curiosity he went to find the master and was invited into the hermitage. The dwelling was furnished with only a table, two chairs, and a bed. "Where is your other furniture?" the visitor inquired. "Where is yours?" the master asked in return. Bewildered, the man answered, "I have no furniture; I'm just passing through." "So am I," responded the master. Good religion reminds me that because I am passing through this life, I am called to embrace its reality with an awareness that "we have no lasting city here."

The more I recognize and honor the truths embodied in other religious traditions, the more difficult it becomes to see my own as the one true church, outside of which there is no salvation. Good religion recognizes the common spiritual bond that unites all people. It is less parochial and more inclusive. It is more concerned with finding common ground with other traditions and less focused on differences. And among its members, who struggle always to embrace its tenets, there is an attempt to communicate rather than a tendency to excommunicate.

As they grow spiritually, many people find it difficult to maintain a connection with organized religion, for the experiences and beliefs that fuel their lives go far beyond the creed, cult, and code that define the meaning and the message of conventional religious thinking. Through posing a series of questions, Jesus scholar Marcus Borg clarifies the focus of religion and religious living in a way that many questioning people find meaningful:

> Is the religious life focused on this life or the next . . . ?
>
> Is it about meeting God's requirements . . . ? Or about living by grace . . . ?
>
> Does it lead to a preoccupation with our own salvation . . . ? Or to a liberation from self-preoccupation?
>
> Does it result in an emphasis on righteousness and boundary drawing? Or is the emphasis on compassion and on inclusive social . . . vision?
>
> Is it about believing in a supernatural being "out there" or about being in relationship with a sacred reality "right here"?[4]

In comments she made after reading a first draft of the manuscript that has become this book, Julia Roller, my editor at HarperSanFrancisco, echoed what others have told me—namely, that unlike many postmodern Christians, I "write with a lack of anger." I hope that is true. I hope I am not angry at institutional religion, though I know that I was for a time in the past. Whether that anger was directed at God, the church, or its hierarchy, I knew I had to acknowledge and experience it in order to be free from it. I had to acknowledge the oppressive effect that the mentality and the actuality of organized religion had had on me personally because I internalized its prohibitive dictates.

Even as a child I had a sense that the church, and all that

went on within its walls, had great significance. I was often bored during liturgies, as were my friends, but beneath the boredom I felt a resonance with something holy that I could not name. Despite this sixth sense, I was not able to shake the fear and guilt that are religion's shadows, and indeed have only recently realized I do not have to; I just need to refuse to give them power to kidnap me from the awareness of the loving presence that is God.

On my good days I no longer feel anger about religion's dark side, nor do I seek the security and comfort that religious practices sometimes offer. What I do seek is to give expression to my own (and to humankind's) deepest longings and beliefs. It is not answers to the unknown that I desire, but a way of relating to what can never be grasped. Thomas Merton, a Trappist monk and poet, spoke to this when he said, "In the progress toward religious understanding, one does not go from answer to answer but from question to question."[5] Religious doctrine can be a problem if we let its answers prevent us from living life's riddles, for it is in this way that we come to a deeper faith. Likewise, we can wrap ourselves in cocoon-like religious devotions that bring such comfort that we never venture forth to confront the difficult and the unknown, and never, therefore, develop into the person we are capable of becoming. But true religion invites us into the heart of Mystery. It calls us to be vulnerable to the Spirit, open to the divine dynamism that, like a smitten lover, longs to captivate our hearts.

Religion concretizes our need to reach beyond ourselves and into the depths of ourselves, where we encounter God. It utilizes symbolic language and teaches values, norms, and rituals in order to give expression to the ultimate nature of existence. Because we are earthbound, bodybound creatures, we require the form, substance, and relationship that religion and church offer; without these we run the risk of spiritualism, the disdaining of the holiness of life in the flesh.

Periodically I encounter people who claim, in the midst of discussions about religion, "I went to the old school!" By this they mean that they learned, and continue to prefer, a traditional/conservative approach to faith. Many of us have spent some time at the "old school"; we know both its teachings and its tenor. However, as we develop an appreciation for the mystical dimension/intention of religion, for its ability to awaken us to our oneness with God and one another, we become students in the "ancient school." Mysticism reaches far back into religious history. Its understanding of God, religion, and faith is prior to, and deeper than, the beliefs and practices that "old schoolers" have become comfortable with. Religion is about our relationship to the Mystery that is beyond dogma, doctrine, and ritual.

Religion is an ambivalent concept for me. I continue to recognize its value and my need for involvement in it, but I no longer feel nurtured by its institutional structure in the way I once did. The understanding of religion that resonates with me has to do with my relationship with the infinite, intimate, and ultimate reality of God incarnate in creation. I continue to engage in the religious practices of my faith tradition, but the most dynamic meaning of religion for me now refers more to a communal living with faith in life's holiness than it does to embracing specific beliefs, participating in worship services, or obeying rules of behavior. The latter are a means to the end that is our oneness with the One in whom we are one.

Meditations

The purpose of the teachings and practices of any religion is to put us in touch again with the truth, so easily lost sight of, that we are one in you O God and one with you. It is one thing to know this and another to express it. I am a religious person not because I belong to a faith-community, but primarily because I am a person whose life bears witness to your presence in me. It is one thing to believe in you, but the extension of that belief into action (worship and compassion) is essential, because we are human. Love for a person remains mere sentiment unless it is expressed. Belief in and love for you is given flesh through religious practice, which involves loving action done in faith.

❧ ❧

Through religious practice and shared teachings and tradition, I am bound to a community that can strengthen my faith and commitment to live counterculturally. To embody the values of the gospel puts me at odds with the self- and success-oriented dictates of society. To be a person of faith is to be homeless on the earth. Good religion reconnects me with the realization that "we have no lasting city here." Humanity is a family uprooted, one that is accompanied by you at the same time that we are moving toward our lasting abode in you.

❧ ❧

Religious loyalties in past and present times have been the source of conflict and bloodshed. In its best and broadest sense, religion binds me not only to those who share my specific faith-tradition, but to all people. Everyone everywhere who senses the longing for you, called by whatever name, is my brother or sister in faith. The bond that religion is meant to give expression to is one that exists between me and all others. It has been said that one Christian is no Christian. But no matter what one's affiliation in terms of a faith-tradition, it is always true that we go to you alone/together. We are individuals in communion with you and in community with one another. To sever the bond with one is to damage the relationship with the other.

Religion is about relationship in the context of Mystery. Because we live in your vastness, our life is not our own. We do not have a relationship with you; we are a relationship with you. We cannot comprehend the utter intimacy from which we arise and in which we live, but we can give expression to it in words and in silence, through gestures and stillness. Religious ritual should incorporate these modes as it celebrates the mystical truth of the one reality that is humanity/Divinity.

Personal Reflections

Chapter 2

Father

Is the Father God? The Father is God and the first Person of the Blessed Trinity.
  A CATECHISM OF CHRISTIAN DOCTRINE

The word "God" is not a proper name. It is not the name of some great big person somewhere "out there." The word "God" functions like x in algebra. It is the stand-in for the mystery.
  MICHAEL J. HIMES,
  DOING THE TRUTH IN LOVE

First impressions are difficult to change; this is as true in the realm of the Divine as it is in the human realm. My first impressions of God came from my traditional Catholic upbringing, but they are probably no different from those conveyed by most religious traditions.

I always looked forward to getting out early on Monday afternoons from Clinton Elementary, the public school I went to in Detroit, Michigan. The early dismissal was allowed so that I could attend Catechism classes at St. Francis de Sales, the nearby Catholic school. It was there that I first encountered formal teachings about God and all things religious from nuns in long, black habits. I absorbed those teachings like a sponge. I learned from them that God was a person—an old, wise, loving, demanding father figure enthroned in heaven. God had created everything, just as it says in the Hebrew scripture's book of Genesis, and he kept a critical eye on it all.

A Catechism of Christian Doctrine, commonly known as the *Baltimore Catechism*, was the text that taught me God was a Supreme Being who was to be known, loved, and served in this life so that I could be happy with him in the next. What I heard in that statement was that God was a physical entity, a person like me, minus the flaws and plus the power. Although I could know, love, and serve God on earth, the sole purpose for doing so had to do with what would happen later. God was sort of here, but really there. The only happiness that mattered happened in heaven.

It was God's job to test my resolve, to strengthen my will, and to try my patience by seeing to it that my life had its share of difficult times and pain-in-the-neck people (a role ably filled, when I was young, by my siblings). In referring to our relationship with such a God, Thomas Merton is said to have used this image: God stands on one side of a great abyss, and we on the other. Stretching between the two cliffs is a two-by-four, thin side up and greased. It is our task to make our precarious way to God by walking on the board, but as we do so God lifts his end and shakes it just to make things interesting. This difficulty and that disappointment were God's doing. These troubles and those heartaches were designed, on purpose, to bring me to my knees and to strengthen my faith.

At best, most of my first impressions of God were a

mixed bag full of love and fear, trust and uncertainty. My teachers did a good job of presenting me with the notion of a God who was made in the image and likeness of humanity, one who was pleased by my compliance on the one hand, but whose anger flared at my failure to toe the line on the other. But no matter how much my actions or failures to act displeased God, he could, like any good father, be cajoled into forgiveness by sincere contrition and a confession of guilt.

Speaking of guilt! Guilt was a pretty constant companion of mine and, I believe, of almost everyone who took God seriously, because to do so was to buy into an ethic of perfection, to strive for the lofty but impossible goal of being without flaw, which inevitably led to frustration and self-judgment. Whether the sensation was intense or subdued, there weren't many days in my youth when there wasn't something to feel guilty about—things I did (disobeying my parents was a biggie, and lying to a nun haunted me for years), or should have done (like being kind to the hearing-and-speech-impaired kid in my neighborhood), thoughts (about girls), feelings (also about girls), thoughts about feelings, feelings about thoughts. I was a pro at guilt. Before I graduated from grade school, I held a Ph.D. in guilt. You name it, I felt bad about it; and I was certain that God felt bad about me.

Thinking back to my youth, I recall words such as *omniscient*, *omnipotent*, and *omnipresent* being used in reference to God. The God I learned about was the all-knowing, all-powerful, ever-present Prime Mover, the first cause and last resort. I learned that God was the *alpha* and the *omega*, both my source and my destiny. Though there is truth conveyed by these notions, that truth felt a little chilly. I found it hard to warm up to an omni anything, and *alpha* and *omega* were Greek to me!

I learned that God was provident, which literally means "seeing before." God, like any good parent, was watchful and protective. I was assured that if I were good, I could count on God's providence and that nothing bad would happen to me or through me. Though I would hesitate to proclaim this to any thinking person now, I was convinced of its truth the day my mother stopped me as I was leaving our house dragging the shotgun my father used for hunting. "Where are you going with that?" she demanded. "I'm going to shoot Terry Kay" (the neighbor girl, who, like me, was about five years old). "Why do you want to shoot her?" my mother asked, understandably troubled. "Because she said I have cavities." It made sense to me at the time.

It's been said that God created mothers because she couldn't be everywhere. My mother was the instrument of God's providence more than once, but I confess that since that day I have secretly hoped that God would relax her providence and allow Terry to experience the joy of at least one root canal.

The impersonal and sometimes negative notions I had of God were first impressions, but they were not lasting ones. I record them here only to supply a contrast to a different understanding—one that has evolved over years through study, experience, and grace. What I learned early on became the bedrock of my current faith: God is a reality; there is more to life than meets the eye. I absorbed the truth that I can communicate with God and that the particulars of the life of every person are of consequence. And I became aware that my deep restlessness, my inability to be content, had something to do with my longing for God.

As much as I value what I was taught in my early years, I find the God of my first impressions no longer believable. That God is too distant and impersonal to be in sync with the intuitions and convictions that tell me God is present, passionate, and personal. The God of my youth, as I have mentioned, was one in relation to whom I often felt guilt. I recall a time when I was in the throes of scrupulosity. I had a thought that grew into a conviction and a resolve: "To hell with God, if he wants me to feel this bad." It was the beginning of liberation. The notion of a more benevolent God did not immediately emerge for me, but from that time to this I have never given credibility to the "God of guilt."

I wish I could say that the sense of guilt that once plagued me is no longer a burden, that its weight has lightened in proportion to my awareness that God is not preoccupied with my imperfection; but the reality is otherwise. Like a storm cloud ready to deliver its payload, a sense of guilt still hovers over me (and, I know, over many others). Some of it is *good* guilt, the voice of conscience that calls us to be our best selves. This is the voice that makes us feel wrong when something fixable is not quite right, or when something possible is within our reluctant reach. But the guilt that is a residual effect of an unfounded fear of God is one that we must learn to live with. When we become convinced that God is the force within that calls us not to be ideal but to be real, and that does not judge our performance but embraces our person, the presence of lingering religious guilt can be accepted—neither acquiesced to nor fought against. For to do either of these is like trying to get a mouthful of water from a tsunami wave—we will surely be overwhelmed.

I have come to realize that most guilt is the result of growth. Imagine yourself as a small child standing inside a box. As long as you do not touch the box—the walls of restriction placed around you by parents, religious authority, and the conventional attitudes of the culture—you feel comfortable, content, guiltless. But as you grow, you become too big for the space. Guilt is what is felt when your body touches the walls of your box. Even *thinking* "outside the box" can feel wrong, but the real wrong, the ultimate tragedy, would be to live small, to fit into rather than outgrow your confines, to recoil with each pang of conscience.

I now believe that God can neither be limited to our likeness nor confined by the inadequacy of our language. Joseph Campbell says this well when he states:

> God is an ambiguous word in our language because it appears to refer to something that is known. But the transcendent is unknowable and unknown. . . . God is beyond names and forms. Meister Eckhart said that the ultimate and highest leave-taking is leaving God for God, leaving your notion of God for an experience of that which transcends all notions.[1]

When I ask people, as I often do during retreats, what has caused their first impressions of God to change, there is a near-universal response. The catalyst for their development and mine has been life itself. When we confront life's inconsistencies with religion's explanations, life wins. The hard and fast reality of life's occurrences, especially those that are harsh or unfair (like the untimely death of a loved one, betrayal by a spouse, or physical, emotional, or sexual abuse by a parent or other authority figure), forces many of us to rethink our theology. If we are to remain people of faith, and if God is to continue to have relevance in our lives, we must think and believe in ways other than we have.

When the traditional notion of God ceases to have meaning, many of us begin to embrace God as a boundless reality unlimited by time, place, or gender. This God is not impersonal, but neither is this God a person. Such an intangible God is beyond imagining and may seem difficult to relate to, but as we move toward a faith worth believing, we are often more compelled by the intangible and paradoxical than by the concrete. Though God is not definable or confinable, God is, at the same time, more real than anything our minds or senses can discern. As reassuring as it would be to know who, what, and where God is, any such knowledge would be false and limiting; it would be to make an idol of an icon, a finite reality out of the infinite Truth. God is not a person apart from me. God is the Ground of who I am. I discover who I am, and how one I am with creation, by being lost in God's Oneness.

Traditional religious teaching tends to quantify and personify God, making him a him! This is reinforced by the use of words such as *Father, King,* and *Lord* in reference to God. When we personify God, we get an image and a handle that enables us to picture and talk about God in ways that are comprehensible; but we limit God in the process. To do otherwise—to refuse to be content with a God of our own making—is to be true, believe it or not, to Christian theology, as theologian Michael Himes indicates:

> We Christians do not believe in a "supreme being" out there someplace. God is not one being among many beings, not even the supreme one. St. Thomas Aquinas taught that God is the power of being, being itself

(esse), but not a being *(ens)*, supreme or otherwise. Thomas made "God" more like a verb than a noun.[2]

To say that the word *God* is verb-like is to understand that God is a life-giving force that moves in and through creation. I believe God, thus understood, to be provident, but not in the sense of being protective, of preventing bad things from happening to good people. We are not provided *for*, but provided *with*, enabled by the force of the Spirit to see the sacredness of what befalls us and to respond to life's circumstances wholeheartedly. God's providence, Being's benevolence, is at work not only when things go our way, but when, in the midst of personal heartbreak or collective tragedy, we recognize that in bad times as well as good, in sickness as well as health, in times of conflict as well as peace, life is holy, and that by surrendering to this truth we become holy ourselves.

I still, despite knowing better, find it difficult to trust in God's providence, to open myself to life and relationships. I know from my own experience, and that of others, that life is unpredictable: anything can happen to anyone at any time. Given this, it is nothing short of an act of faith to engage life fully and to become vulnerable to another. I fear more than anything else the pain that is a broken heart. But if God is the Ground of Being, as I now believe, then it is here—in the loves and losses, the beauty and the battles of our existence in the flesh—that we encounter God.

Having learned to look upon God as a benevolent reality, and having learned not to allow the voice of guilt to have the last word, I no longer strive for perfection (*per facere*, meaning "to be done through"). I now recognize that I am being perfected by life. I am being baked like a turkey in an oven. I am being readied for the great banquet, slowly cooked through by the heat of joys and sorrows, gains and losses, triumphs and tragedies. Perfection is not something I attain; it is the work of the "chef"—it is Divinity's doing that takes place through the holy randomness of life's occurrences.

I do not mean to imply that we are without power or responsibility in shaping our lives. However, our part in the process of being perfected does not involve the willful overcoming of our faults; rather, it involves the faithful entrusting of those faults, and of our whole selves, to the mercy of God.

While I was making a retreat at Genesee Abbey, a Trappist monastery near Rochester, New York, one of the monks told me about a conversation he'd had with the abbot. The monk was speaking about the sense of security he felt in the monastery. The abbot looked both *at* him and *through* him when he said, "Our security is in the mercy of God." Although our efforts are important, they cannot, in themselves, bring about the security or the holiness that we, by nature, desire.

I have come to believe that God is not someone residing in a faraway place whom we must try to please and to whom we must answer for our shortcomings. God is not a person, male or female, who is out to test us. God does not require our perfection or await us only at the end of life. God does not, despite our pleading, protect us from harm. The notion of God that I find most compelling at this point in my life is *panentheistic,* a word that means "all-in-God." Marcus Borg writes about this concept of God:

> God is the encompassing Spirit; we (and everything that is) are in God. . . . God is not a supernatural

being separate from the universe; rather, God (the sacred, Spirit) is a nonmaterial layer or level or dimension of reality all around us. God is more than the universe, yet the universe is in God. Thus, in a special sense, God is not "somewhere else" but "right here."[3]

Author Annie Dillard, quoting theologian David Tracy, says that panentheism is the private view of most Christian intellectuals today. She goes on to say, "Not only is God immanent in everything . . . but more profoundly, everything is in God."[4] Though we may not always be aware of the mystery that is our life in God, we are in God and we incarnate God. This is mysticism, an intimacy with the Infinite here and now—the presence of Presence in the midst of our daily lives.

God is a reality in my life that is less concrete than was once the case, but paradoxically God is also more real to me than ever. The word *God* no longer denotes a supernatural person; it connotes a sacred truth having to do with the divinity of humanity and the holiness of creation. God is for me the spiritual essence that infuses and enfolds all that is.

Meditations

How can you who are no one be so real? I do not and cannot know with my mind what I know in my heart. You, O God, simply are, *though you are not* anyone. *Somehow your Being, which itself does not exist as I exist, is more real than all that exists. Though I know this in my heart, I do not necessarily feel it. What I sense to be true about your presence is a matter of faith—not belief, but faith. That is to say, I surrender my whole self to the truth of your oneness with all that is. I live in the conviction that you who are not, are, and that I who am, am not except in you.*

In thinking, in speaking, in writing about this, I come face to face with the inadequacy of words and images. It is folly to attempt to express the inexpressible or imagine the unimaginable, but not to do so is like not breathing. I cannot not speak of you. I must. *And yet, as a result of the apparently fruitless endeavor to think the unthinkable and give expression to what cannot be put into words, something occurs: the mystery of my communion with you is deepened. You to whom I cannot be more united, I am even more one with. You are closer to me than I am to myself.*

In this union there is less of me—of my conscious, observable self. I am still who I am and how I am; that is, my flaws remain. But at some level, some height or depth that is more real than the real world or my perceivable self, I am lost in your allness. I am infused and enveloped. Your presence is within and around me. I am it. It is me. I am not. I am free. And in this state I sense my connectedness to everyone and everything. The sense of separateness from nature and people that is my normal way of seeing life is an illusion. What is most true about creation, and what unites every aspect of it, is you.

It is not often that I experience communion with you and, in you, with all else. What I sense most often is a restlessness that I know is a longing for you. No thing satisfies me, no one puts to rest my need to rest in you. But something in me keeps looking to this world to gratify that in me that is not of this world. Although all creation is imbued with your Spirit and, therefore, could quell my longing for the Infinite, it does not. I must learn to abide my disquiet and allow it to teach me that my longings are holy and that resting in them, rather than attempting to satisfy them, is the way to the peace I seek.

❧ *Personal Reflections* ❧

Chapter 3
===

Son

*Why is Jesus Christ God? Jesus Christ is God
because He is the only Son of God.*
A CATECHISM OF CHRISTIAN DOCTRINE

*Jesus Christ was not God's entry into human
life. . . . It was this divine involvement in human
history, hidden from the beginning . . . that
was made manifest in Jesus. . . . In Christ is
revealed that the way of God's presence is
incarnation. God acts through the human in
ordinary words and gestures, in interpersonal
relations.*
GREGORY BAUM, MAN BECOMING

Because God is often viewed as a distant, more-than-human reality, many Christians find it easier to relate to Jesus—a flesh-and-blood person who knew the joys and sorrows of the human condition. In and through him they feel connected to God.

And yet, despite the actual, physical personhood of the Jesus I was introduced to in childhood, he was not someone I could cozy up to very well. Jesus was presented as perfect, flawless, "like us in all things except sin"—which meant that he wasn't much like me at all! He was "fully God and fully man," but mostly God. I was taught that Jesus had, from the git-go, the "beatific vision"—that is, a picture of God's glory—ever before him. The only vision I had before me was the television!

Jesus was only *sort* of human, it seemed to me. I was led to believe that, as a child, he always went to bed when he was told to, put his toys away after playing with them, and ate all his veggies. The idea I had of the adult Jesus was that he was the quintessential nice guy, always showing up, Superman-like, in the nick of time to cast out devils and heal the infirm. With characteristic cynicism and humor, Robert Farrar Capon elaborates on this image:

The true paradigm of the ordinary American view of Jesus is Superman: "Faster than a speeding bullet, more powerful than a locomotive, able to leap tall buildings in a single bound. It's Superman! Strange visitor from another planet, who came to earth with powers and abilities far beyond those of mortal men, and who, disguised as Clark Kent, mild-mannered reporter for a great metropolitan newspaper, fights a never ending battle for truth, justice and the American Way." If that isn't popular Christology, I'll eat my hat. Jesus—gentle, meek and mild, but with secret, souped-up, more-than-human insides—bumbles around for thirty-three years, nearly gets himself done in for good by the Kryptonite Kross, but at the last minute, struggles into the phone booth of the Empty Tomb, changes into his Easter suit and with a single bound, leaps back up to the planet Heaven. It's got it all—

including, just so you shouldn't miss the lesson, kiddies: *He never once touches Lois Lane.*[1]

The understanding of Jesus as Superman-like is deeply embedded in the human psyche. It is an heroic archetype that that speaks to our longing for spiritual greatness. Like everyone else I knew in my youth, I put Jesus on a pedestal that elevated him above and beyond the reach of mere mortals. What I didn't realize was that in doing so I made it more difficult to recognize the divine dimension of my own and other's humanity.

Jesus was the "only begotten Son of God," the one and only incarnation of Divinity sent from above, born of a virgin to atone, by his suffering and death, for humanity's sins. This understanding of Jesus is what Marcus Borg refers to as the "popular image," "a divine or semi-divine figure, whose purpose was to die for the sins of the world, and whose life and death open up the possibility of eternal life."[2]

The agony of Jesus' death was not, of course, the end of the story. *Resurrection* is the term used to refer to the belief that Jesus rose from the dead and, subsequently, appeared to his disciples in the flesh until his ascension (his return to heaven)—also in the flesh. In all ways, Jesus was a larger-than-life figure. He was what everyone should be like in life, impossible as that may be, and the one in whose company we would be if we resembled him at the time of our death.

Though his coming was thought to be a great blessing for humanity, his Second Coming was another story. I recall hearing about his return at the end of the world as an ominous event. It was the old "good news, bad news" joke: the former was that Jesus was coming; the latter—he was angry! The Second Coming was about judgment and punishment for everyone who was not without sin—which is to say *everyone*. It was, in the image presented in Matthew 25, about sheep and goats, the righteous and the losers. I was never a big fan of goats, but, in this scenario, I always felt I was in their company. I felt about the Second Coming the way I felt about my father's return home at the end of a day when I had done something deserving of reprimand. Yes, Jesus loved me. Yes, he was my friend. But I kind of liked the idea of not being home when he returned.

Many of my notions of Jesus were fanciful and flawed. He was someone who was approachable, on the one hand; but the closer I was to him, the worse I looked in comparison. Still, I learned, in learning about him, that both his flesh and ours is pretty holy stuff. Though he was a model of perfection I could never attain, I had a sense that I was not alone in my walk through life, and that my humanity had something to do with Divinity. My understanding of Jesus is vastly different now. I see him as more human, but no less holy, and I see myself as more like him, despite my imperfections.

Some years ago, while studying philosophy, I recall having the disturbing realization that I no longer believed most of what I had been taught about Jesus. Surely he was a charismatic and prophetic person, but was he literally God's son? Was he really sent here? Did his death atone for our sins? Despite these questions, I continued to resonate with the ideals he embodied and with the values he espoused, especially his prophetic opposition toward all who inflicted judgment and injustice on others. I was a seminary student at the time, and I wondered how I could continue on that path, given my doubts.

A few years later, in the early 1970s, I continued to grapple with these questions, but now I was on the verge of ordination to the priesthood. One evening I happened to see a television interview with Jesuit priest and peace activist Daniel Berrigan, about his actions in protest of the war in Vietnam. He embodied for me all that I was drawn to in the priesthood and in Jesus. With the prophetic presence of both Jesus and Berrigan as a catalyst, I was able to embrace the priesthood and put my faith in Jesus despite my misgivings about the traditional understanding of his divinity.

The gist of my Christological quandary was articulated by a woman who came to me for spiritual direction. Sharon asked, "Do you think Jesus was sent by God, or did he grow to understand who he was?" I used to think that Jesus was sent with an intact awareness of his identity and purpose: that he knew he was "God's son" and was destined to be the lamb slaughtered and sacrificed to atone for humanity's sinfulness. I now see this and other notions about Jesus as part of the Christian myth, the story we tell, in embellished ways, in order to convey the truth about who he was and who we are in light of him. Jungian analyst James Hillman, in *The Soul's Code*, speaks of the necessity of embellishment in reference to the "genius," the sacred self at the heart of humanity: "I must tell a story of distortions to really tell the truth. The story must be adequate to the exceptionality of the genius."[3]

I believe that Jesus, unlike most of us, developed an awareness of God as abba-like, close, personal, compassionate. I believe that he gradually, but profoundly, grew to have a sense of uniqueness and mission as he became more and more smitten by the communion with God that formed his "genius," his deepest sense of identity. I believe that he, like most of us, struggled to make sense out of this sense of himself, and that he may have tried to escape its inevitability as

did the "Everyman" referred to in Francis Thompson's poem
"The Hound of Heaven":

> I fled Him, down the nights and down the days;
> I fled Him, down the arches of the years;
> I fled Him, down the labyrinthine ways
> Of my own mind; and in the mist of tears.[4]

It is this God-inspired surrender, or cooperation with
grace, that distinguishes Jesus from the rest of humanity in
the eyes of those who believe in him. All of us are called to
cease fleeing and to allow ourselves to be overtaken and
taken over by the ravaging benevolence that consumed
Jesus. But we generally quicken our pace and harden our
hearts to Love's advances.

I recall doing this one night while staying in the hermitage that was the refuge of John Eudes Bamberger, OCSO,
then the abbot at Genesee Abbey. I was near the end of my
first visit to the monastery and had asked permission to
spend a few days in the hermitage. I awoke in the middle of
the night with a profound sense that I was being asked to
"give all," to let go of myself and to be willing to live not by
the dictates of my desires, but by the promptings of grace
and the needs of others. I immediately turned my head and
said a silent but emphatic no. I intuitively sensed, even in my
half-awake state, the radical nature of this invitation. I knew
that surrendering to its wisdom was the way to true happiness, but I also knew that the selflessness involved in going
with it was a kind of death to the only self I knew myself to
be. In an attempt to rationalize my resistance to this call, I
convinced myself that this experience was a case of mistaken
identity: God must have thought I was John Eudes!

Granted, we may be far from perfect because of our reluctance to allow God to claim us, but the essence of who we are is who God is. When we are blinded by the light of Jesus' person, as Christians often are, we fail to see what he himself saw—that everyone, ourselves included, is a dimension of the Divine. But when we see in him our oneness with God, and with one another in God, we may be moved to relate to everyone, Jew and Gentile, slave and free, male and female, gay and straight, etc., with the reverence that is due them.

I have ceased to view certain aspects and events in Jesus' life literally and have found that this has served to make my faith more real, more grounded in the holy Ground of life. What I now believe is less saccharin, but no less sacred.

I now look to, and at, Jesus not exclusively as the "only Son of God," but as the one in whom I recognize that all of us are daughters and sons of the Divine. To take the term *incarnation* seriously in reference to Jesus is basic to Christianity—he was indeed an enfleshment of God. But it is also basic to our faith to take that term *personally*. Jesus, in his having grown to be a person who surrendered fully to the truth that he was "of God," is a revelation of what it means to be a person.

I do not believe, in any literal way, that Jesus was "born of a virgin." Joseph Campbell claims that the myths of many cultures at the time of Jesus (and since) told of the virgin births of their heroes. The writers of the gospels used this image to communicate their conviction that Jesus was no ordinary man and that he, not Caesar—about whom the claim of a virgin birth was also made—was their Lord. To say that Jesus came from somewhere else and that he was conceived in a humanly impossible manner was a way of indicating his stature, his place of prominence, and the power of his purpose.

In like manner, I do not believe, as I once did, that Jesus' resurrection was a physical phenomenon, but I do believe that it was both real and powerful. Mark Twain once said: "The older I get the more vividly I remember things that never happened!" In looking at the life of Jesus, and at his resurrection in particular, I think we can say, "Just because it didn't happen doesn't mean it isn't true." The truth of the resurrection lies in the experience of his disciples then and now. The power of his presence was and is experienced by those who believe in him. The resurrection, in this sense, is both historical and hysterical. The former—an historical event—happened, though it was not a *physical* event: his presence was truly in the midst of his followers even after his death. The latter—an hysterical event—is happening still: that vital presence is real, it is felt, it is personal, and it is powerful today. Jesus' resurrection understood as an hysterical truth is a call to rise from the graves in which we lie lifeless, depressed, paralyzed by fears and insecurities.

It is a resurrection of sorts when, fueled by a sense of the Spirit's call, a man who is held in the grip of addiction takes the first halting step on the road to sobriety. Or, again, when a woman afflicted with depression begins a regimen of medication and exercise. Or when a couple, discovering that they are strangers in an empty nest, begin the often painful process of reconnecting, perhaps with the help of a counselor. The historical resurrection of Jesus is an inspiring story about something that occurred in the past. Hysterical resurrections are inspiring events that take place every day.

I realize the claim that Jesus' resurrection was not a physical occurrence may sound heretical to those who read scripture literally. But for many others, faith in Jesus' divinity is not dependent upon the events in his life or on miracles attributed to him. Rather, it has everything to do with surrendering to the Spirit that inspired him. Strange as it may sound, Christian theology has never claimed that Jesus rose from the dead. The claim is that he *was raised* from the dead. The distinction is not merely semantic, for the latter affirms that the one Spirit that enlivened him and each of us is unquenchable, victorious even over death itself.

It is hard to imagine anyone calling him- or herself a Christian but not believing in the atonement, Jesus' redemptive death on the cross. But even this doctrine stands on shaky ground. I have had to dig deep beneath its surface soil in order to discover and embrace its hidden truth. There is little doubt that Jesus was crucified, but there is plenty of discussion in theological circles about the why and wherefore of his death. The fact that the early followers of Jesus were largely Jewish makes it reasonable to believe that they looked at him and at his life through the filter of their faith-tradition. Jesus was seen as the scapegoat on whom were heaped the sins of the community, the one sent out to die so others could live. He was seen as the "Lamb of God" whose blood, like that of the slain lamb in the Exodus story, saved the innocent from death.

I no longer believe that Jesus' death "opened the gates of heaven," or that he saved me from eternal damnation. If this were so, God would be someone made in my image and like-ness—namely, one who required appeasement as a criterion for forgiveness and mercy. I believe that Jesus' death was the result of his ruthless pursuit and articulation of the truth that God is greater than religion, that love is higher than the law, and that compassion is more important than purity. In living and preaching this, Jesus was at odds with the religious power structure of his culture. It was elements of this structure, in conjunction with Roman civil authorities, that put Jesus to death.

Despite the fact that Jesus' death did not open heaven's proverbial gates, it was redemptive for his followers then, and is so for us now, if we allow it to open our eyes to the truth that a certain type of death is necessary if we are to be fully alive. In an archetypal sense Jesus' death is an atonement in that it invites us to live in "at-one-ment" with God. If I am true to the Truth in me, if I surrender to the Spirit that breathes in me, if I live in a way that is congruent with that Spirit (loving, giving, forgiving), then the death of my ego-self that takes place in this faithfulness to being my true self enables me to enter the kingdom that is here and now.

This reading of Jesus' death and atonement suggests a different understanding of the Second Coming/end of the world. Rather than a cataclysmic condemnation, the Second Coming may be a compassionate completion that takes place for each of us to the degree that we undergo the redemptive death to what is false in us and come face to face in ourselves with the Christ we have come to resemble in our selflessness. When this becomes the reality of our lives, we see that the kingdom of God is not a future state of affairs but a present reality, a view supported by Campbell:

> What is the meaning of the End of the World? The denotation is that there is going to be a terrific cosmic calamity and the physical world is going to end. . . .
>
> The Kingdom of the Father is spread upon the earth, and men do not see it. Not seeing it, we live in

the world as though it were not the Kingdom. Seeing the Kingdom—that is the End of the World.[5]

Jesus continues to be significant for me now, as has always been the case. I no longer view him as someone magically born and blessed, but as a Spirit-filled, flesh-and-blood epiphany of humanity's divinity. I do not believe that he was sent from heaven, but that he heeded the interior call that sent him to the center of himself, wherein he discovered God. He is not the one and only Son of God, but the one who awakens me to the truth of my oneness with God, the one who saves me from the sin/death that consists of living in ignorance of the divinity of humanity. In this sense he is truly the savior of all who put their faith in him (that is, entrust their lives to him).

Meditations

Jesus, who are you to me now if you are no longer who I thought you were in the past? Although I see you as more human, you are no less divine in my eyes. In you I recognize that humanity is blessed. I recognize in your flesh the truth that God was in the beginning, is now, and forevermore will be the soul of my self and that of every person. What I discover in you is the incarnation of God in me. What I realize in your being who you are—one who is one with God—is my own (and humanity's) identity.

Your person calls me to something. Because I see in you what it means to be alive with God, I feel compelled to surrender myself to the Spirit, to die to the inclination that would have me live a small life, one focused exclusively on myself and on those who like, and are like, me. In you I understand that to become in word and deed the incarnation of God—the incarnation that I am by nature—I must respond to everyone with a reverence that honors their divinity. To be alive in and with God compels me to live in relationship not only with the in-dwelling Spirit, but with the Spirit enfleshed in my friend and my foe, in my known neighbor and in the neighbor who is a stranger to me. There is such a thing as appropriate boundaries in relationships, but there are no borders when it comes to life in your Spirit.

In the past I thought that to be a Christian meant to be a good person—that is, to do no harm, to help those in need, and to live a life of purity and piety. I now realize that more is required; for you were, along with being a peacemaker, a troublemaker. Although I fear the consequences of doing so, I cannot not be prophetic as you were. Whether aiming toward the secular culture or the ecclesiastical structure, I know I must challenge the status quo and resist the gravitational pull to fit in. Whether focused on myself or on my relationships with others, if I am true to what it means to live as you lived, I must challenge the inclination to rest content with anything less than honesty and integrity.

I may no longer believe literally all that is said of you in the scriptures, but I hold to the truth that those stories convey and I feel the dynamism that drove you to live fully, to die courageously, and to be raised spiritually. In your life, death, and resurrection I recognize the myth, the eternal and archetypal story, that beckons to the heart of our humanity. All are called by our spiritual nature to experience in our own unique way the power that moves us to live, to die, and to live again in the many ways this process occurs this side of the grave.

Personal Reflections

.

Chapter 4

Holy Ghost

Who is the Holy Ghost? The Holy Ghost is God and the third Person of the Blessed Trinity.

A CATECHISM OF CHRISTIAN DOCTRINE

Perhaps most people think of the Holy Spirit as the most shadowy member of the Divine Trinity. . . . If we remember that the Spirit is God . . . then we also understand that He is God at his closest to us.

JOHN MACQUARRIE,
PRINCIPLES OF CHRISTIAN THEOLOGY

The Holy Ghost, I learned in childhood, was the third person of the Blessed Trinity, the Father and Son being the other two. The Trinity was pictured as a triangle; the Holy Ghost was depicted as a bird—a dove.

The term "Holy Ghost" always struck me as an oxymoron. How could something be holy and ghostly at the same time, since ghosts were scary (except for Casper), and holiness was a step or two above awesome?

In any case, I was never quite sure where the Holy Ghost was or how to grasp its meaning and purpose. This made the image of a bird appropriate, for unless such a creature is wounded or otherwise immobile, catching hold of it is almost impossible. Birds soar beyond reach; they belong to the sky. Though I didn't know it when I was young, both birds and the Holy Ghost speak to the spiritual dimension of our humanity.

The three-personed God I learned about became more concrete for me when I was told of their three corresponding functions: the Father created, the Son redeemed, and the Holy Ghost enlivened and unified. My best handle on this aspect of the Holy Ghost was conveyed by the feast of Pentecost. Originally a pagan agricultural festival celebrating the firstfruits of the grain harvest, Pentecost was adapted by the Hebrew people as a remembrance of the giving of the law to Moses. Pentecost in the Christian tradition refers to the coming of the Holy Ghost to the apostles in the form of a strong wind and tongues of fire. The effect of this event was that a group of fearful men and women huddled together for safety became fearless preachers whose words could be understood by people of every race and nation. Although the Holy Ghost was not a reality I could relate to very well, the impact of it on Jesus' followers was appealing. I liked the idea of being fearlessly on fire—and being understood by anyone, much less everyone, was a plus.

I recall learning that Pentecost was considered the birthday of the church. Apparently *something*—I didn't know what it was—had come into being when Jesus' apostles were visited by the Holy Ghost. This didn't make a lot of sense to my child-mind, since the apostles had already been born and since, at that time in my life, I associated the word *church* with a building. Although the events of Pentecost helped to clarify my confusion about the Holy Ghost, the notion of its being a birthday served to recloud the picture.

I was excited when I realized that I too could receive the Holy Ghost in the sacrament of Confirmation. When I was growing up, this sacrament was conferred at about age twelve; it was supposed to be an initiation into spiritual adulthood, as is the bar/bat mitzvah of a Jewish child. My excitement was tempered by fear. I, and the others in my class, had been warned that the bishop who would preside at the ceremony would ask us questions from the *Baltimore Catechism*. How embarrassing it would be for us, and for the nun who taught us, if we didn't know the answers. Another source of fear was that we had been told the bishop would ceremonially slap us on the cheek as a sign that we had to be tough in order to defend the faith. Not really taking in the word *ceremonially*, I braced myself for the big hit—which, to my relief, turned out to be a mere tap.

At Confirmation you became a "soldier for Christ," you took on a new name—that of a saint you admired—and you chose a sponsor, someone whom you looked up to and who modeled the maturity you were about to assume. The name I chose for myself was Joseph, which was Jesus' father's first name and my father's middle name. My sponsor was my cousin Francis, who gave me my first watch to mark the solemnity of the occasion. I loved that watch; it was beautiful and, I thought, expensive. I wore it until it stopped running about three weeks later!

There were other kinds of gifts associated with the Holy Ghost—seven to be exact: wisdom, understanding, counsel, fortitude, knowledge, piety, and fear of the Lord. I was already in possession of the latter long before I was confirmed. The others are still in process; like time-release medication, they take effect little by little.

At the time I was learning about the third person of the Blessed Trinity, that subject played a distant third to sports and girls. However, the vague sense I had of the Holy Ghost when I was a child became more real as I grew not only to understand, but also to experience, the fact that "real" was not necessarily synonymous with "material." I came to sense that my thoughts and feelings about the Holy Ghost were not only real to me, but that they related to an unseen reality both within and beyond me. They were not fabrications of mind and heart, for their reality was dependent upon the spiritual actuality of that to which they referred.

I cannot identify any particular incident that occasioned this new consciousness, for it is the nature of the Spirit to be elusive. But I gradually began to sense within myself a Presence that was more than myself. And in relation to the world and other people, I felt a bond that I intuitively knew was of God. I felt that I was one with everyone and everything in the allness of God. I sensed that this was not a common experience, and I knew enough not to mention it during ballgames or in mixed company. But it began to dawn on me that what had occupied third place in my life was beginning to take precedence over any- and everything else. It occurred to me that I, like Jesus' disciples, might have been visited by the Holy Ghost.

The Holy *Ghost* is now referred to as the Holy *Spirit* within the Catholic Church, and the term *Blessed* Trinity has given way to *Holy* Trinity. Despite changes in terminology, I am not much clearer now on the meaning of the Trinity than I was as a child, but I have come up with a notion that makes simple sense to me. Theologians may wince at this distillation of the Trinity, but I see it as referring to the three-dimensional whereabouts of God: the Father is God beyond us (transcendent), the Son is God among us (immanent), and the Spirit is God within us (intimate). The Spirit (*anima* in Latin, which is also the word for *breath*) is the animating force, the enlivening presence of God that breathes in every living being. It is not a ghostly presence hovering ominously, but the benevolent core of who we are. I learned early on that people are temples of the Holy Spirit, and now I understand the truth of that claim: the Spirit is the Life of our life, the Pentecostal breath of God both within and beyond us.

We sometimes use the term "free spirit" when talking about someone who is his or her own person. Free spirits are people who think for themselves and act on their beliefs and intuitions, no matter how others might react. They are not necessarily insensitive, but they often live by the adage "Ready, fire, aim!" Free-spirited people are fun-loving and life-affirming; they can also be wonderfully irreverent. We can easily assume that Spirit-filled people are pious people—careful in word and gentle in action, measured and moderate in all things. But precisely because the Spirit is free, those who do not allow it to be confined by convention or dominated by decorum are delightfully unpredictable. By their manner of living they give witness to the boundless nature of the Spirit, as did the wannabe nun, Maria, in the musical *The Sound of Music*, who was too full of life to fit into the structured existence of a convent. She could easily be labeled unorthodox but, in reality, she was a paradox—so filled with the energy of the Spirit that in order to obey God she had to disobey the limiting dictates of her religious superior.

Perhaps the most free-spirited person I have ever known was my father. It would be a stretch to call him religious, but he exuded the Spirit. He was uninhibited in communicating his thoughts and feelings, he loved life and people, he had a terrific sense of humor, and, before Parkinson's disease and other ailments began to take their toll (and eventually his life), he was absolutely at home in all aspects of his body (physical, emotional, mental). When the Spirit inhabits us without the constrictions of self-conscious insecurity, we become, like my father, naturals at living life and, at times, breaking rules.

For a free spirit, rules are made to be broken, a truth my father delighted in. On one occasion he was in the swimming pool of the building in Florida where he and my mother owned a condominium. He paid no attention to a sign that indicated he had to wear a bathing cap when in the pool. As he was treading water one day, an angry resident of the building swam toward him and voiced the fact that he was not in compliance with the rules. My father continued to tread water as he apologized profusely—urinating all the while! He enjoyed telling this story, but keep in mind that free spirits sometimes stretch the truth for comic effect.

As I have changed spiritually, so has my understanding of Pentecost, which I now view as the celebration of an inspiration that has moved humanity from the beginning. This insight was confirmed for me by religious educator Michael Morwood, who wrote:

In the Pentecost experience . . . the followers of Jesus came to a clear belief and awareness that the same Spirit they had seen in Jesus was present and active in their lives. They came to believe that this "Spirit" could be as courageously expressed in their lives as Jesus had allowed it to be in his life.

Was the presence of the Spirit of God in their lives a new phenomenon conferred only by Jesus returning to heaven and "sending the Spirit"?...

We can continue to understand the experience of Pentecost as the granting of the Spirit in a special way or we can understand it in the belief that God's Spirit has never been absent from any aspect of creation.[1]

The firestorm of God's enlivening presence has always breathed life into our hearts. Pentecost is about the inspiring, God-filled energy, not always felt but always real, that has never ceased moving us to act in the face of fear, to have faith in the midst of doubt, and to live freely in the apparent confinement of our commitments and responsibilities.

I experienced the Spirit's inspiration most recently while writing this book. I'm not talking about an energy flowing through me that made the process of writing effortless. On the contrary, it was when writing was most difficult, and when I wanted to abandon the task, that I felt a force within that enabled me to stay the laborious course.

The inspiration of the Spirit moves us to act faithfully and freely, but its force is tempered by our human limitations. The disciples, though alive with the Spirit, remained as human after Pentecost as they were prior to it. In the same way we, despite the fact that we are temples of the Holy Spirit, remain broken beings who manage to manifest God in the midst of our stumbling. The authors of scripture, though inspired to relate the truth, were very human and were influenced by a variety of factors, both personal and cultural, that make the Bible a document that must be read critically rather than literally in order to be accurately understood. The Bible is a product of inspiration, not dictation, and although its communication of God's truth is not verbatim, it has a reliability that is not jeopardized by the human hand or mind of its various authors.

Pentecost is about God's unrelenting and inspiring "with-us-ness"—not only individually, but collectively as well. The Spirit is at work not only, or even primarily, when an athlete performs beyond her or his personal best, but when the whole team does so. An inspired actor is a joy to behold, but an inspired cast has an even greater power to move our hearts. It is hard to imagine anything more beautiful than the well-trained voice of a singer, unless it is the harmonious blending of an entire chorus. The unifying function of the Spirit challenges and enables us to go beyond the development of our individual selves to the formation of our communal selves, wherein we recognize and revel in the full unity that honors our diversity.

In the days before Pentecost Jesus' followers were not open to the validity of all paths to God, for they were Jews who loved their tradition and considered it to be the one right way to be religious. I now see that the church was born, and began to be truly catholic (universal), when that fearful band of believers in Jesus ceased to be concerned for their safety, and when they began to move beyond their Jewishness to embrace all people. I think it is safe to say that the church is in constant need of rebirth because it tends, as do all institutions, to think in terms of survival and maintenance of the status quo rather than in terms of being faithful to the spirit of the gospel no matter what the cost.

The question that gets to the heart of the need for rebirth

is: "Are we a church with a mission, or a mission with a church?" If the emphasis is on *church*, the Spirit is easily stifled by concerns about orthodoxy, liturgical correctness, clerical privilege, compliance with authority, and the like. The child-abuse scandal that is ravaging the Catholic Church as I write, and the clerical culture that has resulted in the cover-up of this situation, could be a reality only because the institutional character of the church has overshadowed the mission of the church. The conflict between the Missouri Synod and the Evangelical Lutheran Church of America is also reflective of this phenomenon, as are the battles fought over the ordination of women and gays and the lines drawn between Christian denominations because of their differing views regarding the Eucharist. When the predominant focus of a church is with its own internal order, it is probably less alive than it could be.

But if *mission* is prominent, if the task of embracing and embodying the gospel is not compromised by too great a focus on maintaining the system, the Spirit's transforming power will be unleashed and the structure of the church will become a means, not an end. The wind and flame that symbolize the Spirit's presence will, like a blazing forest fire, destroy what needs to die so that new growth and vitality may occur.

I have seen this phenomenon at work in the Catholic diocese of Saginaw, Michigan, where I facilitated a retreat for lay people training to assume leadership roles in their parishes. These included not only established roles involving distribution of the Eucharist, lectoring, and visitations to the homebound, but also presiding and preaching—areas usually, and even officially, restricted to the clergy. I could feel the Spirit's energy during the weekend I spent with these people: they were empowered and powerful in a way I have rarely witnessed.

It is human nature to resist the destruction of what is familiar, comfortable, and secure. Because religious beliefs and practices are all those things for many people, change within religious institutions is always slow going. But if the Holy Spirit is alive and well, the winds of change will continue to blow and its "living flame of love" will never be quenched. Openness to the transforming Spirit will ensure that "the Way," as the movement that formed around Jesus was originally called, will never become "the Stay"!

I once felt the Holy Ghost to be a "shadowy member" of the Trinity, a dimension of the Godhead that defied images and concepts. But it is precisely the undefinable/unconfinable character of the Spirit that appeals to me now. The Holy Spirit, like wind and fire, is a powerful force bringing about sometimes painful change and promoting necessary growth. The Spirit is the dynamic nature of God at work in all creation.

Meditations

I can no longer say the words or pray the prayer I once addressed to you—"Come, Holy Spirit"—for I now realize that you are here already. Your life and your power fill the room in which I sit and the person that I am. It is your being that enlivens me and your power that moves me to live with passion. To say "Come" to you now is to ask you to break through my blindness to your presence. It is to invite you to take hold of me every time I lose sight of you in myself, in others, and in nature. You do not come where you are not; you become real to my senses and my soul here, where you have always been and will always be.

Because humanity is your temple, your dwelling place, I am bonded to everyone who is, was, and will be. It saddens me when the pull of my own ego and the beckoning presence of my needs and desires cause me to lose sight of you in me, and the connection I have with other people in you. The dimension of myself that imagines me to be separate and distinct needs to die. Your function in life is to enliven and unite. If I am less than alive, and if I live at odds with myself and others, I am not experiencing the fullness of your power and presence.

How can I so often feel lifeless when you, life itself, are the bot-
tom line of my being? Perhaps my need is not to feel alive, but to
realize that I am alive in you even when I do not feel it. I will
always prefer the consolation of your felt presence over the
absence of feeling. But awareness, whether of the head or the
heart, is less important than the sheer reality of being alive with
your life. I do not have to be conscious of, or rejoice in, the fact
that I am breathing in order to be enlivened by that function.
You are the breath of life that sustains my soul whether I am
aware of it or not. My life is greatly enriched by conscious
awareness and felt feelings, but before, beyond, and beneath my
experience of you, you are in me and I am in you.

You are not only within me but beyond as well. You are not only
an embodied phenomenon but also a boundless one. I encounter
you in stirrings and in stillness, in the sound of thunder and in
the sounds of silence, in the company of others and in solitude, in
what is and in what is not, in being and in nothingness, in time
and in timelessness, in the particular and in the general, in the
common and in the cosmic. You are present in failure as well as
success, in sickness and in health, in confusion and in clarity, in
death and in life

Personal Reflections

Chapter 5

The Self

What is man? Man is a creature composed of body and soul, and made to the image and likeness of God.
    A CATECHISM OF CHRISTIAN DOCTRINE

My being is encompassed within Being itself. The mystery of the Self is part and parcel of the mystery of Being.
        SAM KEEN, HYMNS TO AN
            UNKNOWN GOD

My only regret in life is that I'm not someone else." In these few words Woody Allen, exaggerating for comic effect, articulates an attitude of self-deprecation that afflicts most of us at various times in our lives. If only I were more intelligent, outgoing, attractive, wealthy, etc., I would be happy with myself. It is not a difficult task for most of us to identify the characteristics of our personality, our biology, or our circumstances that we wish were different; in fact, many of us tend to focus on these and spend a large portion of our time and energy trying to change them.

65

In my religious formation I got the impression that in order to be pleasing to God I'd better become someone else—someone less rebellious and more compliant, less sinful and more holy, less human and more angelic. Of course, I was taught that I was made in God's image and that I was a temple of the Holy Spirit, but what seemed even more true was that sin had the upper hand; the temple was in need of cleansing and repair. I felt that I had to do battle with myself; I had to conquer the enemy that was me.

The gist of the message that I received concerning myself was one of mistrust. Without constant vigilance my very own nature would betray me and lead me away from goodness and God. I was more a child of Adam than of God, and being so I lived in separation and alienation from my source and destiny. This is what is meant by referring to human nature as "fallen." Original sin, which according to the biblical story has its origin in Adam and Eve's decision to eat the fruit of the tree of all knowledge, is our most defining characteristic. Our progenitor's very names—Adam from the Hebrew *Adham*, meaning "humankind," and Eve, meaning "mother of all living"—suggest the far-reachingness of their sin. We are inclined toward evil and are in constant danger of falling prey to pride.

I was taught that pride was the first and the worst of the seven so-called *capital sins:* covetousness, lust, anger, gluttony, envy, and sloth are the others. With *pride* defined as "too high an esteem of oneself," the worst thing you could do was to be proud of your accomplishments or appearance; this was like broadcasting to the world that you were teetering on the brink of hell. It was always important to do and to look your best, but if you thought you were hot stuff, you'd better keep it to yourself.

One effect of the emphasis on the self as fallen is expressed well in the journals of Etty Hillesum, a Dutch Jew who died at Auschwitz: "It is difficult to be on equally good terms with God and your body."[1] I learned that to be a person is to be at odds with God, because to be a person is to have a body, and to have a body is to have needs, physical and emotional, that demand attention. To attend to our needs is good to a point, but a person can easily become overindulgent. I got the impression that our bodies were a bit like baggage: we toted them around, but they kept us from moving full speed ahead spiritually. We would be better off without them.

When I was growing up, the dimension of our bodily being that was considered most problematic had to do with sexuality. Although I knew it not to be the case, it always felt to me that church teachings had more loopholes for someone who committed a felony than for those who entertained sexual—a.k.a. dirty—thoughts! The shadow of impurity hovered over all thoughts and actions of a sexual nature. Only in the sacrosanct commitment of marriage was sex considered holy—and even then not as holy as celibacy.

Despite the existence of "the Index," a list compiled by the Catholic Church of books that were not to be read (usually because of their sexual content), and the forbidding of "B" movies for the same reason, the church's attempt to protect adolescents from exposure to things sexual served only to heighten curiosity. I'm sure that my friends and I were no different than most kids when we were young; the majority of us were naïve and inexperienced, though we pretended to know more than we did whenever the topic of sex was raised—which was about every five minutes. Make that three! But there were always one or two who really knew what they were talking about; they had enough dirt in their minds to apply for statehood. Being in the know about sex was problematic because, although not being wise or experienced in this arena made you uncool, knowing too much at an early age made you suspect in the church's eyes.

There was more than a kernel of truth in what I learned about myself in relation to God. There is a dimension of me that resists God and fears the very intimacy for which I long. It would be naïve to assume that without effort I could live in full cooperation with grace and in total union with my God-self—that deep, spiritual identity that names the truth Jesus embodied; namely, that there is a sacredness to the self I truly am beneath the surface of the self I think I am. Although it made me overly vigilant and self-critical, what I learned about myself has helped me to recognize that I can easily undermine my own happiness and that I must, therefore, be appropriately self-conscious in order not to be self-defeating.

I have come to view the story of our fall from grace not as literal but as metaphorical. The Garden of Eden is an image for our self at one with God. It is a "place" we inhabit but have lost touch with. We live out of sync with the truth of God's indwelling. Psychoanalyst Jean Bolen writes about this phenomenon: "When an individual lacks the inner sense of being connected to God . . . a wound exists that the person experiences as gnawing, pervasive, persisting insecurity."[2] Though we are born with this wound, it is deepened by experiences such as abuse, neglect, and abandonment. These give rise to a slew of self-defeating behaviors that reinforce the conviction that we are of little worth in God's eyes—or anyone else's, for that matter. I have come to believe that it is not pride but blindness to our oneness with God—a blindness that issues in a proclivity to self-negativity—that is our original sin. Just as Adam and Eve, upon eating the apple, are said to be aware of their nakedness, so most of us are burdened with a lingering consciousness of our imperfections and shortcomings, the inadequacy of our very selves. It is difficult to love ourselves or to let others love us when the inner voice of criticism and insecurity reigns.

I was struck recently by a sense of the universality of this condition while speaking with Emily, an attractive and competent young woman who, for her entire life, has attempted to earn the love of others. Despite her diligence, she has never felt as if her efforts were satisfactory—no matter how hard she works, no matter how praiseworthy her accomplishments, she continues to feel inadequate and driven to produce and to succeed. My suggestion that what she was doing was good enough because *she was good enough* was as difficult for her to imagine in her life as it is for me to imagine in mine. Although she recognizes the importance of self-affirmation, and has made strides toward it, Emily, like most of us, continues to grapple with the demons of self-negativity.

I am in need of constant reminders to keep me from being too self-critical. One of those helpful reminders took place while I was speaking with my spiritual director. I was bemoaning, or perhaps whining about, the fact that I was not the person I wanted to be. I was not who I could be or should be. I felt that I was letting God down and that I was ill-equipped to take on the challenges life was bringing my way. In her firm and loving way, Rose looked at me and said,

"Everyone is dealt a winning hand. The only way to lose is to fold, to give up and to give in to the negative voice of self-criticism." What she was saying was true—I *could* be better, holier, more generous, and so forth; but if I played my cards wisely, if I gave life my best shot, I would be a winner.

After the "fall," the Genesis story says, God went in search of Adam and Eve. I used to think that God was seeking them out for the purpose of blame and punishment, but I now believe it was to embrace them and to communicate an undying love. In doing so God would have done well to cite these words that adorned the front of a birthday card I received years ago: "You are amazing grace. You are a precious jewel. You—special miraculous unrepeatable, fragile, fearful, tender, lost sparkling ruby emerald jewel rainbow splendor person."

Words as loving and tender as these can be hard to hear when we feel that we have abandoned the garden of God's presence. Life in the world often feels like an exile, but the reality is not that we exist apart from God, but that we exist in a state of forgetfulness of God's nearness and of our dearness to God. "Our birth," William Wordsworth writes in "Intimations of Immortality," "is but a sleep and a forgetting." Forgetfulness of this sort seems to come with the territory of our existence and is, therefore, a fairly constant state. However, it can also be a periodic intruder that rains on the parade of a felt sense of God's presence. In this case our forgetfulness can be viewed as a "dark night of the soul," the dry, empty, confusing experience of having lost our way to God. Dark nights are painful times for anyone who seeks the Divine, but they are important because they strip us of the illusion that feeling close to God is an indication that we have "arrived." Just as it is true that "the Tao that is known is not the Tao," so it is true that no feeling of God is God.

Despite the presence of sin understood as our being out of touch with God's indwelling, we do not live isolated from God, for our very self is an incarnation of God. We are sacraments of the Divine, the means by which the transcendent God is manifest. There is no denying the truth that we are most often out of touch with our God-self, and that we must exercise watchfulness and discipline to stay in tune with this dimension of ourselves. However, our existence and identity derive from God; we cannot be apart from God and live. "Let it be known from East to West that apart from me there is no one," God proclaims (Isa. 45:6). It is natural to be frustrated and critical of our inability to live in a way that is consistent with our best self, but it is never accurate to assume that we exist in a state that is other than one of intimacy with God. Thomas Merton knew the truth of our inherent oneness with God:

> Since our inmost "I" is the perfect image of God, then when that "I" awakens, he finds within himself the Presence of Him Whose image he is. And, by a paradox beyond all human expression, God and the soul seem to have but one single "I". They are . . . as though one single person.[3]

This statement is based on a theology that is radically incarnational. God's being is given expression in humanity. This is not a denial of the transcendence of God, but an affirmation of the truth that transcendence and immanence, Divinity and humanity, are not separate. The mystery that is

God is all-pervasive. We are, with all our flaws, a source of wonder. The fullness of God unfolds in us when we are lost in God, one with the Life that lives in and through us.

When we forget that God's glory lives in our aliveness, we seek glory, directly or indirectly, of a different sort. For two years in the early 1990s I lived in Rolling Prairie, Indiana, in a cabin situated on a small lake surrounded by woods. The one oddity in this idyllic environment was that my closest neighbor was Oprah Winfrey. "The Farm," as she calls it, is an estate that serves as her respite from the hectic pace of life in Chicago, a little over an hour away. I would sometimes find myself daydreaming about meeting and becoming friends with Oprah. I realized that my fantasy came from my desire to share in her glory. It was about my not valuing myself enough: I wanted to become someone special by knowing someone who was special. I never did meet her, but I did introduce myself to Stedman Graham, her significant other. Impressed?

The conviction that our essential self, the person beneath the persona, is an expression of God can free us from the burden of both self-hatred and self-inflation. There speaks in most of us a persistent inner voice that would have us believe that we are hypocritical whenever we resolve to do the right and lofty thing. It is quick to remind us of our hidden self-interest even in the most altruistic endeavors. A similar voice tries to convince us that we are being magnanimous when, in fact, we are only paying lip-service to others' needs without paying the true price of love—the willingness to die to our comfort and preferences. But when we know (are intimate with) the radical union with God in which we live, no voice reigns in us except that of Love, which says, in the words of Merton scholar James Finley, "My life is yours and your life is mine. Our unity is who you are."[4] Being convinced of this truth enables us to remain constant and confident in the midst of turmoil, connects us with our rootedness in God, and enables us to proclaim that, no matter what we've been taught to believe, there was never anything wrong with us, despite the fact that we have not been, are not now, nor ever will be perfect.

Despite having developed a more incarnate understanding of God and of the sacredness of ourselves, many of us continue to grapple with our bodies. Our culture bombards us with images and verbal messages that tell us our bodies must be youthful, thin, and beautiful. The religion I grew up with indicated that having a body was a problem. Today's culture tells us our body is a problem only if it doesn't look good.

And yet our bodies are essential to our holiness. We are embodied spirits. We cannot deny our physical and emotional needs and expect our souls to thrive. But neither can we cater to them as entities independent of the Spirit without running the risk of becoming enslaved to their needs.

The mature way to relate to our physical selves is the way of celebration. We rejoice in the wonder that is the human body. We give thanks for its amazing strength and delicacy. We respect its limits and honor its capabilities. If our bodies could speak for themselves, they might say, in the words of poet Edward Galeano:

> The Church says: The body is a sin.
> Science says: The body is a machine.
> Advertising says: The body is a business.
> The body says: I am a fiesta.[5]

Though I once felt myself to be, by nature, at odds with God, I now recognize that I am a unique expression of the Divine. Beneath the tangible aspects of my being that must be embraced despite their imperfection, I am in communion with "I Am." The Self of my self, the essence of humanity, is the holiness of God.

Meditations

The true measure of growth in the spiritual life has to do with awareness of the holiness of humanity. It is a long road to journey from a sense of self as primarily flawed to one that is first and foremost holy. I so easily return to the starting point. I fall back into a pattern of thinking and feeling that makes you, O God, a distant and demanding figure and see myself as one who must strive to please and appease you. What a far cry this is from arrival at the truth of the oneness with you that is my soul. I do not have to overcome my imperfections to be in union with you. My holiness has nothing to do with me, but has everything to do with the presence in me of the Holy. My task is not to please you, but to gently and compassionately live in accord with my true/holy/God-self.

Although I am convinced that I cannot and do not exist apart from you, I know that the awareness of this truth visits me only fleetingly. I would like it to be otherwise. I want always to walk with the full awareness that I walk in you, but I also know that it is somehow right that I forget this. I must grope in the darkness, the not-knowing and not-feeling, if I am to learn to walk and to dance with Divinity. It is in the darkness that I am led to see a light that is brighter than I have seen before. Every time I experience the loss of you, I am invited into the free-fall that takes me to a new depth of relationship with you.

To trust this and to remain open to its possibilities issues in my becoming myself in a new, more full, and more holy sense.

To know my nothingness is to know my holiness. I have no existence apart from you, from whose Being I derive. To imagine myself apart from you is an illusion. The reality of my being is a statement about your Being. The reality of my nothingness apart from you is a commentary on the fact that my life is sacred. The point of human life is not to become someone—albeit someone good, loving, holy, etc.; it is to be the "no one" we truly are—lost in you, one with the All. Our true identity is not our self, but our Self; not the wave but the sacred sea from which it has arisen. When self-consciousness becomes Self-consciousness, I become aware of the expansiveness of who I am in you.

The process of my becoming someone who is no one (myself lost in your allness) is none of my business! I cannot consciously attain the status of being one with you. In fact, striving for this is a proclamation of my ignorance of the truth that that union is already a reality. But what I can do is be open to the fact that by striving to attain this state my ego can be undone. My limited understanding of myself as someone striving to be one with you can be transformed by the futility of the striving into the explosive awareness (enlightenment) that I am not separate from that which I strive to be in union with. To arrive at this realization, this experience of freedom and aliveness, is the fruit not of my efforts but of your grace.

❧ Personal Reflections ❧

Chapter 6

God's Will

For what do we pray when we say "thy will be done on earth as it is in heaven? . . . We pray that all men may obey God on earth as willingly as the saints and angels obey Him in Heaven.

A CATECHISM OF CHRISTIAN DOCTRINE

God's will is not the will of some other person out there someplace with which we are supposed to bring our will into line. The will of God is the will within and beneath my will.

MICHAEL J. HIMES,
DOING THE TRUTH IN LOVE

There was never any doubt in my mind that the God I grew up believing in had a very definite idea about how things should be, and a clear preference, though not always clear to me, about how that ideal was to be attained. This notion had a name: it was "God's will." God's will had to do with the world being a peaceful place, with relationships being loving, with our remaining free from sin, and with the discovery of what it was we should do with our lives.

Moving from the general to the particular, God had something specific in mind for me (and you) about everything. God's will was an agenda that was for my own good, whether I knew it or not. My task was one of discernment and obedience. I had to figure out God's will and fall into line with it. A cloud of obligation and conformity hung heavy over the notion of God's will. There was but one right path to walk; to not discover it was to be lost. James Finley relates, with humor, an instance in his life that expresses this understanding:

> To discern God's will doesn't mean to discern a particular course of action. Three years ago I had to make this decision. I was trying to decide whether to move to Pittsburgh or to move to South Bend—we were living in Cleveland. So I thought about it and thought about it, and prayed about it and prayed about it. And I decided to move to South Bend. Now it isn't as though maybe it was God's will that I move to Pittsburgh, and so maybe He's still waiting for me in Pittsburgh at the airport, and the last three years are completely invalid—God doesn't know where in the hell I am![1]

If God's will was not about discerning a particular course of action, nobody told me. The one thing I was pretty sure of, however, was that God's will was probably the opposite of mine. I was certain, for instance, that it was God's will, as well as my mother's, that I learn to like liver and that I get good grades in school, neither of which happened—ever!

The more difficult something was, the higher it was on God's "Things for Tom to Do" list.

I learned that doing God's will meant conforming to the norms and dictates of my faith-tradition. I didn't always have a clear sense of what God wanted of me, but if I stayed within the "fold," I knew I couldn't go too far wrong. In this case, it was God's will that I believe what my religion taught, that I worship at the times and places it required, and that I act in accord with its rules of behavior. There was no guess-work here, no gray area to ponder, no discernment necessary. What there was was certitude and security. I knew when I was in the right and when I was not, when I had complied with the will of God and when I had turned from it.

The notion of God's will was also a way of explaining the unexplainable. How was it that a virtuous person could fall, Job-like, on hard times, while the lowlifes of this world prospered? Answer: it was God's will. Only God knew the wisdom behind life's travesties and tragedies. What was certain was that they were not pointless; they were just beyond my ability to comprehend.

It is no secret to anyone who has lived an examined life that God's ways are not our ways. My idea of the best way to get from one place to another, be it in terms of geography or of biography (i.e., becoming who I think I should be), is a straight line—no detours, setbacks, or interruptions allowed. What usually occurs is everything I wish would *not*, but somehow this turns out to be the best way of all, a way full of growth and new discoveries. The way that is not my way is God's will at work shaping me, through the frustration of my designs, into a more perfect likeness of the Divine.

It was the realization that there is a grand benevolence at work in life even when things go awry that laid the foundation for what I now believe about God's will. Though I had come to fear the possibility of not knowing God's designs for me, it was comforting to know that I didn't walk alone. I was not just one of the masses God had created; I was someone for whom God cared enough to have a plan. This conviction, though narrow compared to my current understanding, was essential for openness to a more dynamic interpretation. The question I once asked, "What am I supposed to do?" is different from, but related to, the question I now ask, "Who am I to become through the circumstances that surround me, the people I relate to, and the decisions I am called upon to make?"

I now chafe at a rigid understanding of God's will, for it is inconsistent with my belief that God is the Spirit that breathes in me. I have come to believe that God's will is not an agenda that, should I misread or ignore it, would lead to a life of unhappiness or an eternity of condemnation. God's will is not what God wants, but what God WANTS! Not, that is, God's preference, but God's passion, desire, or longing, as Robert Farrar Capon indicates:

> The will of God now becomes, not the order of a superior directing what a subordinate must do, but the longing of a lover for what the beloved is. It is a desire, not for a performance, but for a person; a wish not that the beloved will be obedient, but that she will be herself—the self that is already loved to distraction.[2]

It was not many years ago, while reading *Hunting the Divine Fox*, the book just quoted, that I had the "aha" experience that freed me from an understanding of God's will as the imposition of an agenda. I had taught, counseled, and preached that God was a benevolent reality that embraced us as we were (broken), while at the same time inviting us to wholeness. But the felt sense of that truth touched me only when I discovered that "willing" is an ingredient of "loving" (to love is to will the good of the other), and that God's love is for me first and for my actions only secondarily. What I do matters because I matter.

An important caveat to this is the realization that just because I happen to be the apple of God's eye, and just because I happen to love God back, doesn't mean that whatever I do is blessed by God. I am not aligned with the true meaning of St. Augustine's statement "Love God and do what you will" unless my love for God moves me to do, objectively, what is in the best interest of myself and others.

The application of my current understanding of God's will is one in which I am almost constantly engaged as I attempt to discern whether to remain a priest. At one level I feel that I should do so, that I am supposed to, because I vowed myself to that life for a lifetime. Surely this faithfulness to a commitment made must be the will of God. But when I consider God's will not as a plan I must discover and conform to, but as a loving presence present in me that moves me toward a holy wholeness, the picture becomes less clear. Can I be fully alive in the life I have chosen? Am I able, through that life, to enable others to embrace their lives with passion? Am I being true to who I truly am and not just pleasing others or reaching for an ideal that leaves what is real in me unacknowledged or unattended? When I cease to relegate God to a distant heaven and God's will to a blueprint for my life, life with its many decisions becomes more muddled. However, I need not fear taking a wrong turn, for Love itself accompanies me whether I end up in Pittsburgh or South Bend!

Like any lover, God is consumed with the beloved. We are the apple of God's eye. The term "God's will" is a way of speaking about the love affair that is the Divine/human communion. God's will is not something we do; it is God's nature. God is the desire that is at the heart of our hearts. To surrender to the will of God thus understood is to allow ourselves to be loved and possessed by God, to be consumed in the fire of Passion itself, and to be conduits of it to all who cross our path.

It has been said that God's will is what is. To achieve a union of wills with God is to say yes to life as it is and to myself as I am, flaws included, for God's desire for us is not dependent on perfection or beauty or any other standard by which we typically measure. "God's ways are not our ways," as we often hear.

This saying is known to everyone who has been influenced by mainline religious teachings. We generally presume that God's way, or will, has to do with our perfection, spiritually and otherwise. God wants us to attain the ideal. What I have come to discover is that perfection is *our* way, not God's. We strive to become our ideal self, thinking that to achieve less renders us unacceptable to God, to others, and to ourselves. God's way/will, paradoxically, is less demanding. It is, I believe, that we learn to love and accept ourselves as we are. This is the necessary foundation for any lasting change.

The older I get the more I am convinced that much of what occurs in life is unexplainable, especially events that are difficult to accept. Just before writing this I left the bedside of a woman named Nancy, whom I visited in my role as

a hospital chaplain. At forty-five, Nancy is partially paralyzed, blind, and in constant pain. She is a mystery to the
medical profession: not one of the many doctors she has con-
sulted has been able to give either a diagnosis or a prognosis.
It is understandable that she would ask, as she did, "Why
me?" and that she would bargain with God for a cure, even
though she doesn't believe in a God who intervenes in life. I
wished I had a comforting response to her "Why me?" but I
knew it was a question of the heart not the head, and that it
required my presence, not my answer. As inadequate as I felt
just being there, Nancy seemed to appreciate my presence
(as I know I would have appreciated hers).

"It's God's will" is not an appropriate or a true response
to this situation, or to similar situations (no matter what a
person's beliefs may be), for there is no predetermined reason for circumstances such as this. There is, however, a
reason of another sort: the reason anything and everything
occurs is who we become through its happening. Whether
now or later, whether in ways that are dramatic or subtle, all
of us are visited from time to time with afflictions that test
our mettle. How we enter into the sorrows as well as the joys
of our own and others' lives determines whether we grow or
not, whether we mature spiritually or linger unenlightened
through the course of our lives. The desire of God for us and
in us has everything to do with our development as whole
persons, and therefore with our willingness to engage reality
whether we like it or not.

I may not be able to grasp God's ways in the midst of
life's difficulties, but I am learning to trust that I am in God's
grasp no matter what. Though I no longer believe that God's
will is anything and everything I wish would *not* happen, I
have come to see the "hand of God" in happenings that are

not to my liking. When my penchant for order is frustrated by life's messiness, I am being invited to "Let go and let God." When my desire to be alone is interrupted by the immediacy of another's need, I am being summoned to freedom from my desire. When my ability to function in a way that gains the affirmation I long for is interrupted by sickness or injury, I am given the opportunity to realize that my worth as a person is not dependent upon what I do. And when I am confronted with the necessity of having to communicate hard things to people I love, I must die to my desire to be liked and risk the possibility that both I and my words may be rejected. In all these situations (and in others like them), the will/desire of God is at work through relationships and events, bringing me, if I embrace them, to a new depth of spiritual maturity.

As we grow spiritually, we become more aware of the demands of life in the world and of God's presence in the fabric of the ordinary. Though God's will may not be considered an agenda for every decision or circumstance, it has significance for the details of the everyday. How we maneuver through life and relationships, how we work and play, can be done in a manner that is in keeping with the divine longing or in a way that opposes it. We can be open or closed, forgiving or grudge-holding, compassionate in relation to all that unfolds or resistant to all that does not comply with our will.

I no longer strive to discover what God, understood as a Supreme Being, wants me to do with my life; but I do attempt to be vulnerable to the "inner voice," the usually subtle intuitions that are the God-inspired movements of my deepest self. I try to listen to what excites my heart and I honor what limits my body, for these are indications of how I ought to live, what I should or should not do if I am to live in accord with the desire of the Divine. God's will is that which inclines me out of love to live in a manner that is right for me, given my physical and emotional makeup, my temperament, my talents, my "soul's code."

In other words, I can know (be at one with) God's will by being attuned to myself. However, this needs to be broadened lest the notion of God's will become an excuse for doing only what feels right or fulfilling for me. I must, along with being attuned to myself, be attuned to my Self—the divine depth that is more than the physical/emotional me. It is here, beneath all else, that I am one with all others in God. Because we live our lives in the midst of other lives, the freedom to be ourselves is tempered by the reality of the common good. God's desire is for *us* as well as for *me*. I can be certain that I am aligned with God's will when who I am and how I live enhance the lives of those with whom I share this planet.

Meditations

Can it be that there is no one right way that I must discover and follow in order to be aligned with your will? Am I really free to choose to live as I want to rather than as I should? If your will is Divinity's desire, and if you desire me, then what is important is that I do whatever I do wholeheartedly, for this is the way of growth, the way of maturing into the fullness of myself. Life presents me with countless opportunities, only some of which I prefer, to realize my potential. By engaging in life's ups and downs rather than absenting myself from them or attempting to control them, I position myself to be shaped into a person in the fullest sense of the word, one through whom your compassionate presence is manifest.

I used to think that St. Augustine's injunction to "Love God and do what you will" meant that, as long as I had warm feelings for you, I could live any way I pleased. I now assign a different meaning to both aspects of that phrase. Loving you means orienting my whole self toward the sacredness that lies at the core of creation. As I grow in the ability to be moved by life's holiness, what I choose to do will be in accord with it. Therefore, I love you whenever I choose to do what I do in a way that is consistent with the sacred nature of people and of the planet. I am in accord with your will when I live with reverence toward myself,

others, and the environment, and when I refuse to do harm to anyone or anything.

Although I often do battle with your in an attempt to control my life, I am never apart from your will. My resistance and rebellion unfold within the embrace of the Mystery whose reality includes me. I cannot begin to understand how it is that at my worst I remain the apple of your eye. I imagine that I can reject you, but how can I turn from what I consist of? I am captive to your will, but it is a sweet captivity, for it is my liberation.

You desire all without distinction. You are the longing that sustains others as well as myself, for we are all essentially the same, each one of us being an enfleshment of the one Spirit. But I am also known in my uniqueness, and the entirety of your love inspires me as if no one else existed. Your will is personally universal, a reality that is the bond that informs and embraces all creation and every creature. I am in union with your will when I cease to be at odds with my neighbor and myself, and when I share in your divine passion that desires the good of all.

Personal Reflections

Chapter 7

Faith

What is faith? Faith is the virtue by which we firmly believe all the truths God has revealed, on the word of God revealing them, who can neither deceive nor be deceived.

A CATECHISM OF CHRISTIAN DOCTRINE

Faith is not a theoretical affirmation of something uncertain. . . . Faith is not an opinion but a state. It is the state of being grasped by the power of being which transcends everything that is and in which everything that is participates.

PAUL TILLICH, THE COURAGE TO BE

It has been said of the people of our culture that we have been inoculated with just enough Christianity to make us immune to the real thing. Reflecting on my own life, I would say that, harsh as that statement is, it is true. I had just enough religion (rules and ritual) and belief (in doctrine and dogma) injected into my veins to protect me from the dis-ease of faith—the surrender of myself to God in and through a life of loving service to others. Spiritual writer Thomas Moore makes it clear that inoculation of this sort is a problem:

> We can keep faith in a bubble of belief so that we don't see it having direct relevance in day-to-day living. I've worked with several people who are very devoted to religion and pride themselves on their faith. But they have no trust in themselves, and they don't entrust themselves to life. In fact, they use their belief system to keep life at a distance.[1]

The bubble of belief in which I was raised taught me that faith was one of three theological virtues, hope and charity being the other two. Faith was synonymous with membership in a specific religious tradition. I myself belonged to the Catholic faith. Faith implied knowledge of and ascent to the teachings and traditions of my church—and observance of its rituals; the latter were to be attended "faithfully." This was another notion of faith that was part of my immunization. Whether it referred to participation in religious practice or exclusivity in marriage, faithfulness was thought to mean steadfastness, constancy through thick and thin. Fidelity truly is an important aspect of mature faith, but I have learned that one can be faithful without being faith-filled.

Faith was a matter of both quantity and quality in my early church years. I always felt that I should have more of it, and that it should be stronger. If I had enough faith, the gospel said, I would be able to move mountains. Since there were no mountains where I grew up (Detroit), I could not measure the amount I had, but I could judge the *quality* of my faith, which I deemed weak when I gave in to temptation and strong when I resisted it. Another gauge of faith's quantity and quality had to do with feelings of consolation. If in the midst of hard times I felt God's closeness, I could rest assured that my faith was sufficient.

The term "blind faith" was one that I heard often in my youth. My impression was that blind faith was the epitome of faith. It was the unquestioned acceptance of God's existence, the embracing, without doubt, of all that the church taught regarding God. Though great minds had created proofs for the existence of God, all a person of blind faith needed was the word of the church that God did indeed exist. Blind faith was uninterested in, and impervious to, the importance of the age of rocks (the contribution of science to our understanding of creation); what mattered was holding fast to the Rock of Ages.

When it came to matters of faith, there was no room for doubt. A true believer affirmed the mystery of that which appeared incongruous with the dictates of the church. It was the realm of theologians to debate, for instance, why bad things happened to good people; the "faithful" were not to question such things. Skepticism was a small step away from agnosticism, and from there one could get a clear view of atheism!

It is little wonder, as I look back on it now, that the "crisis of faith" I experienced while in college was more than an intellectual questioning of what I had believed about God, Jesus, and other aspects of religion. It was something I experienced on an emotional level as well: fear, anxiety, and insecurity accompanied my doubts. What sense did life make now that the matrix of beliefs that had given it meaning were crumbling? Why bother to live a moral life if reward and punishment were not, as I had once believed, what the afterlife held in store? It was years before I learned that *living* the questions, not *answering* them, was what true faith required. My ongoing attempt to do that—to live the questions—has, I think, brought me to a deeper capacity to live life in a way that is open to God. *This* is the point of faith.

Another term that planted in me a misperception about faith was the "deposit of faith" that was the core of the Catholic Church's teaching. All that was true and necessary for salvation had already been given to Catholicism for safekeeping. This deposit was a body of knowledge, whole and complete, that in part served to distinguish the Catholic religion from other traditions. The meaning of these truths was not always understood fully, but its deciphering, not its totality, was all that was lacking. God's self-revelation was complete.

Despite its limitations and narrow focus, I am grateful for the early introduction I received to faith. Without the ability to believe in a reality beyond what is sensible and comprehensible, people experience life as limited and find their humanity stifled. It is natural to want to quantify and understand that which is beyond our grasp, but unless we can affirm its reality in the first place, we can never grow to recognize that faith has a meaning both more infinite and more intimate than we imagined.

As we mature spiritually, we recoil at the thought of being inoculated. Our best self hungers for the truth no matter how disturbing. Better to be dis-eased and alive than immunized and half-dead. Better to grapple with faith than to settle for belief.

Although true faith is a far cry from believing everything we're taught about God, it is actually very close to the true meaning of the word *believe,* as Marcus Borg indicates: "*Believe* did not originally mean believing a set of doctrines or teachings: in both Greek and Latin its root means to give one's heart to. The heart is the self at its deepest level."[2]

When we give our heart to another, we hold nothing back. Mature faith involves the fearful, exciting surrender of our whole self to God. It is a way of life that requires dying to our ego, to that dimension of ourselves that likes to be in charge, that wants to call the shots, and that cannot, therefore, venture into the murky waters of the unknown with confidence (*con fides,* meaning "with faith"), trusting that, like the Israelites passing through the Red Sea, all will be well even if we get wet.

I don't know about you, but I don't like to "get wet." I want to know what's coming and that I'll be able to maneuver any obstacles before I even set out on the journey. This has always been so for me in the arenas of work, education, relationships, and even God. Control is something most of us like to have, but it is the one thing there is no room for in a life of faith.

Faith has more to do with God incarnate in life and relationships than it does with affirming the existence of a Supreme Being. This is so because God is not absent from the realm of the human and the ordinary, as philosophy professor Dick Westley points out: "Faith is not a way of knowing things which lie beyond the world of human experience. It is rather a way of seeing the deepest reality delivered to us in and by human experience."[3]

The gospel story about "doubting Thomas" (John 20:24) speaks to the connection between faith and life in the flesh. Thomas's faith was weak not because he refused to believe, without seeing and touching his beloved Lord, that Jesus had been raised from the dead. His faith was weak because he refused to open his heart, to become vulnerable, to enter into relationship with Jesus again. When the fear of being hurt causes us to shrink from the give-and-take of relationships, we withhold ourselves from God enfleshed in others. In other words, emotional isolation is not merely a psychological concern, but also a theological problem. If faith is the giving of our hearts to God, and if God is the essence of our humanity, then withholding ourselves from relationships is a form of atheism.

Faith in God incarnate in people is about seeing into the heart of humanity. To recognize the sacredness of everyone and everything is "sighted faith" as opposed to "blind faith." People with sighted faith know that they, and all others, are one with and in God. Faith of this sort opens our eyes to our true identity. We are not, in the words of Teilhard de Chardin, human beings having a spiritual experience; we are spiritual beings having a human experience. We are, at the deepest dimension of ourselves, utterly interdependent with one another in God.

Sighted faith is disturbing because seeing what the eyes of faith behold can challenge us to move from a passive affirmation of God's presence to a hands-on response to it. This was the message addressed to a gathering of students and faculty at St. Bonaventure's College by Catherine Dougherty. She had been a baroness in Russia prior to the revolution of 1917. She came to the United States a pauper and eventually founded Friendship House, a place of refuge for the poor of Harlem. Her faith propelled her into the lives of the poor because she could see both herself and God in them. Thomas Merton was in the audience the night she spoke at the college; he recorded her words in his autobiography, *The Seven*

Storey Mountain: "For, she said, if Catholics were able to see Harlem, as they ought to see it, with the eyes of faith, they would not be able to stay away from such a place."[4] Blind faith affirms the existence of God without the benefit of proof. Sighted faith recognizes and responds to the "hundred proof" presence of God in the flesh.

When we develop spiritually, there is no confusing faith with faithfulness, for the latter, as Merton pointed out, is sometimes an obstacle to true faith: "Fidelity to tedious and predictable rule can become an easy substitute for fidelity, in openness and risk, to the unpredictable word."[5] True faith is a life adventure, a willingness to respond to a predictably unpredictable God whose Spirit moves us in ways that are often confounding but always work for our benefit.

When, for reasons unexplainable even to herself, a woman calls off her engagement to a man only to discover, years later, a partner better suited to be her spouse, she has entered into, and experienced the joy of, living in faith. When a man leaves a successful career to pursue his bliss as, for instance, an actor, he has embarked on a faith-journey and is successful as a person no matter what the outcome. Faith calls us beyond the predictable, the expected, the comfortable. It invites us to be true to the deepest stirrings of our hearts, those intuitions that resonate with the ultimate purpose of our existence and that refuse to be dominated or co-opted by the conventions of the culture, whether civil or ecclesial.

In order to discern these deep movements of the Spirit, we must spend some time in silence, for the noise created by a too-busy life can inhibit our ability to hear with the "ear of the heart." In order to distinguish the voice of God from that of less reliable guides, we must entrust to the wisdom of another person (a soul mate, spiritual director, friend, etc.) what we intuit to be from God.

I found both silent listening and sharing with a spiritual director helpful when I was attempting to discern, and to follow in faith, God's guidance as I grappled with whether to take a leave of absence from the priesthood. I had been ordained for five years but felt unsettled about who I was as a person. The expectations and stereotypes associated with being a priest made it difficult for me to feel and to act in ways that didn't fit the mold. What was I to do with feelings of anger, with the energy of sexuality, with questions about, and conflicts with, the Catholic Church?

As I sat with my confusion, I did not achieve clarity of thought, but I had a sort of sixth-sense conviction. I realized that I had to step out of my role in order to embrace the person who had chosen it. Despite this intuitive clarity, I remained paralyzed until I shared with my spiritual director, at that time a man named Morton Kelsey, a dream I'd had, one in which I'd attended a priest's funeral and climbed atop his casket. Morton's certitude about the obvious meaning of this dream helped me move beyond my fears and take the first step in what would be a three-year journey of faith.

Feelings can be confusing when it comes to faith. I have come to recognize that true faith is not about feeling God's closeness, but about embracing life with its up and downs when God seems more absent than present. While I was visiting with a patient suffering a serious illness, she commented on her lack of a felt sense of God: "I wish my faith was as strong now as it was when I was a child," she said. I told her that she probably hadn't had *faith* when she'd felt close to God; she'd had *feelings*. In the same way that love can become a reality only when infatuation ceases, so too, mature faith becomes possible only when consolation is absent. Faith is not about living with a felt sense of consolation based on the belief in God's existence; it is about living with the conviction, made evident by our attitudes and actions, that everything that comes to pass does so in the mystery to which the word *God* refers.

In the spiritual journey that has been my life, I have come to realize that faith is not a body of beliefs to which I give assent; rather, it is putting my body where my beliefs are. Faith is the wholehearted giving of myself to God's ongoing self-revelation. Every moment of my life is filled with God. Every sight and sound, every person and experience, is a doorway to the Divine. Faith calls us to be fully present and vulnerable to life in all its ordinariness, since the reality of God is communicated through everything.

The faith of my youth was a comforting set of beliefs that gave me answers before I had any questions. I now feel that I live with faith even though, or perhaps because, I no longer believe much of what I once held as true. I attempt daily to give myself to the mystery that is God incarnate in the holy, random wonder of life and relationships.

Meditations

Faith is the willingness to entrust our lives to you. It is a yes said with our bodies, our minds, and our hearts. It is a way of living that recognizes the depth of ordinary existence and moves us to enter wholeheartedly into each moment, every event, all relationships. Faith is a response to the recognition that "in God we live and move and exist" (Acts 17:28). It is living in gratitude for what is, and with a willingness to respond to the inner urges and intuitions through which you speak, and to the external demands that are your dictates.

It is true that faith empowers me to live fully, but prior to its power to move me, faith has to do with my identity. To say that I am a person of faith is to say that I am one who lives in the belief that I have no reality apart from you. Faith involves a radical interdependence with you, for every breath and heartbeat is the gift of you who create me moment by moment. Faith introduces me to the divine depths that underlie my humanity and form the foundation of all that is. Faith opens me to see and to live "beneath" my ego-self and in communion with your indwelling Spirit. It enables me to live "beyond" myself and in communion with your Spirit embodied in all creation.

Faith is an openness to the unknown. It is a willingness to walk in the darkness, to proceed in life without certainty. Faith does not preclude fear; it enables us to act in the face of fear. It is not the opposite of doubt; rather, it invites us to entertain and examine all that appears inconsistent with our inherited beliefs. Faith is not an unwavering adherence to a way of life, but a radical interfacing with the unpredictable changes and chances of life itself, and with the commitments we make along life's way.

❧ ☙

The opposite of faith is not doubt, but control. I seek always to be in control of life. I do whatever I can whenever I can to assure predictability. To live with faith involves dying to the self that wants to run the show. Faith asks me to trust that all that occurs in life, no matter how random, how unjust, how hurtful, how disastrous, is not without purpose. Everything is something that, if entered into with an open mind and heart, can mold and shape us into stronger, wiser, holier, more compassionate people. When I live with faith, I move though life with gracefulness, not resistant to, but accepting of, what is. This does not imply acquiescence to what might be harmful to myself or others, but requires the willingness to acknowledge the reality of evil, to engage its existence, and to do what I can to lessen its impact.

❧ *Personal Reflections* ☙

Chapter 8

Hope

What is hope? Hope is the virtue by which we firmly trust that God, who is all-powerful and faithful to His promises, will in His mercy give us eternal happiness and the means to obtain it.
CATECHISM OF CHRISTIAN DOCTRINE

Hope is not the conviction that something will turn out well, but the certainty that something makes sense regardless of how it turns out. It is hope, above all, which gives us the strength to live and continually try new things.
KATHY COFFEY, *DANCING IN THE MARGINS*

As a child, I learned the Catechism definition of hope that appears above, but in reality I made no distinction between hoping and wishing. I hoped for eternal life after my death, and I made a wish on my birthday that I would get a bicycle for Christmas. To be hopeful was to believe that what I wanted was possible; God and Santa Claus had the power to fulfill my desires, to make my dreams a reality, to make my hopes and wishes come true.

Hope was the virtue that was oriented toward the future. I hoped for what I did not possess, for what might be. The pinnacle of hope was optimism, the undying belief that the future would outdo the past, that darkness would give way to light, that good would prevail over evil.

A hopeful person was the eternal optimist, one who always looked on the bright side and expected the best of all possible outcomes, no matter how dire the circumstance. Frankly, I was never too fond of people who were always positive and cheery. I saw them as Pollyanna-like and unrealistic, living with their heads in the clouds, busy rearranging the deck chairs on the *Titanic!* In their unrelenting enthusiasm, they made me feel like the grim reaper, ready to throw in the towel on life.

Perhaps it was this experience in my formative years that caused me to become leery of the cheery, a sober realist at an early age. During the summer when I was about seven years old, a girl moved into my neighborhood who caught my fancy. She lived a block from my house—that was doable. She could throw a baseball—definitely important common ground. She would be going to my school—almost too good to be true. But then came the crushing realization that turned my hopefulness into hopelessness—she was a year older than I, a chasm which at that age is only a little short of the distance between the north and south rims of the Grand Canyon!

Living the virtue of hope was like walking a tightrope. On either side of the thin line were two ways a person could sin against hope: presumption and despair. The former occurred when you trusted that you could be saved by your own efforts without God's help, or by God's help without your efforts. In order not to be presumptuous I tried to live by the adage "Pray to God for help, but row like hell for shore," or its Islamic equivalent, "Trust Allah, but tie your camel to a post." In my youth I was more a pray-er than a rower, for though I tried like hell to row—that is, to live a sinless life and to be focused on others—I tired easily, drifted a lot, and ended up on my knees pleading for God's help and mercy.

I learned that if I could muster up enough hopefulness, I could win the battle against despair, the tendency to give up and to see all efforts as futile. The desperate person asks, "Why bother? What's the point of trying? Nothing I do will make any difference." Hope was the fuel that kept me going in the face of insurmountable odds. It was what enabled me to endure hard times, to "take a licking and keep on ticking," in the words of the old Timex watch commercial.

I was taught, in my youth, that despair was not just a failing but an out-and-out sin, because it involves not only giving up on the ability to change, but also (according to *Catechism*) deliberately refusing to trust that God will help us save our soul. Despair of this sort is not so much giving up on God as it is coming to the conclusion that I'm not deserving of whatever effort God could put forth on my behalf. It is believing that something I did or didn't do has resulted in my being *persona non grata* in God's eyes—not a status that makes for a lighthearted walk through life.

To be truthful, I often feel as if God is displeased with me. On my best days a lingering sense of insufficiency haunts me. I feel that because of my compromises, my holding back, my refusal to "let go and let God," I have fallen short of God's expectations. Good friends and spiritual directors have enabled me to affirm my worth and to embrace this near-despair, transforming it into an opportunity to marvel at the truth that giving up on God and devaluing myself are one and the same.

Although I tended to view hoping and wishing as synonymous in younger days, I am now aware that the seeds of a deeper truth were germinating within me. And despite the fact that the hope of rowing to shore often seemed hopeless back then, I know now that living in the tension between presumption and despair was preparing me to recognize that God is in the boat with me. What I was taught about the virtue of hope opened me to the fact that there is a dimension to life that is more vast than my limited faculties can perceive. I presumed this larger reality was in the future only, but at least I had a sense of it. Having this belief gave perspective to life and created in me an attitude of wonder that left room for a new understanding of hope.

There is more to hope than believing that this life will get better or that the next life will outshine this one. Hope's strength, firmness, and power rest in the belief that God is ever present and faithful. Hopeful people are undaunted in the midst of adversity, not because they believe things will turn out for the best, but because they are convinced that here and now life is happening as it ought to, by the dictates and in the presence of a Wisdom that is pure goodness.

"Whatever is happening should be happening" is a Buddhist saying that gives voice to this truth. It is easier to agree with this statement when things are going our way, or when they are consistent with our notion of a just God. But affirming it in hard times, in the midst of personal tragedy (loss, addiction, depression) or collective travesty (war, famine, epidemics), allows us to enter the reality of life wholeheartedly. Hope does not involve either the denial of evil or its glorification; it involves a kind of sacred insanity that is willing to affirm that there is meaning in the madness. The mystery of God is in the mess. Without hope based on the knowledge (intimacy) of God's presence, life's randomness eventually drains our spirit, making existence more a chore than a challenge, a burden rather than the blessing it is.

There is something of a future orientation to hope, but it has to do with vision, not with wishful thinking. Hope is born from the hidden holiness incarnate in all creation; it is the offspring of Mystery. Hope knows there is always more to life than the present, and that if what is possible is to become a reality, human effort is necessary. This notion is given expression by author Rick Fields in the dictum "A vision without a task is a dream. A task without a vision is drudgery. A vision and a task is the hope of the world."[1] The vision associated with hope is not about seeing what can be, but about glimpsing a subtle sacredness in what is, no matter how dark and difficult life may be. The task of a hopeful person is not a solitary work, but a cooperative effort carried out in union with the abiding mystery we call God. Merton states this succinctly in what has become known as "A Letter to a Young Activist": "The real hope, then, is not in something we think we can do, but in God who is making something good out of it in some way we can not see."[2]

It has been said that pessimists are people who have spent too much time around optimists! Surely, as we mature in faith, we tend to see the proverbial glass as half-full, but as Benedictine monk David Steindl-Rast points out, hope may be more akin to pessimism than optimism:

> Some people imagine that hope is the highest degree of optimism, a kind of super-optimism. . . . A far more accurate picture would be that hope happens when

the bottom drops out of our pessimism. We have nowhere to fall but into the ultimate reality of God's motherly caring.[3]

True hope is always related to belief in the constancy of God's motherly embrace. The awareness that there is a divine presence that can "break our fall" rescues hope from being synonymous with optimism and places it in the arena of courage, where it belongs.

It is hope at work when a woman, despite her fear and insecurity, reenters the workforce after years spent raising her family. It is hope enfleshed when a man with a terminal diagnosis refuses to give up on life but instead continues, without denial of his circumstance, to pursue his goals with all the energy he can muster. And it is hope when a person carrying the wounds of a relationship gone sour chooses to become vulnerable again for the sake of living life to the full. Hope is not wishing things were different; it is choosing to make the most of our lives given the given—that is, accepting the reality of our circumstances and the reality that the strength of a "motherly" presence accompanies us.

I sense this hopeful, nurturing presence in Mother Nature as well as in human nature. I see it especially in the rebirth that is the season of spring. Nature teaches us that the winters of our discontent, failure, and loss are not as lifeless as they appear. Within the stems and branches of our being resides the undying wherewithal to be born again, and with each new spring there can be a sense that life is even better than it was before.

I experienced the brand of hope I now embrace while on the faith-journey mentioned in the previous chapter. I spent the first year of a three-year leave of absence from the priesthood in San Francisco. As I neared my destination after days of driving, I felt both excitement and panic. I had, years earlier, lived in Berkeley, across the bay from San Francisco. I had friends there, but I had no job now. I had places to stay, but I had no home. I had ideas about how life would unfold for me, but I had no certitude that my ideas would come to pass.

Despite my fears and the gnawing sense that perhaps I should have remained who and where I had been, I felt that I couldn't fail even if I failed to arrive at the clarity I sought about myself. It was *right* to have ventured forth. I was living in sync with the Spirit. What would happen was less important than the fact that I was living from my heart. I was not so much hopeful about what might happen as I was hope-*filled*. I was not alone, even though I was by myself.

I was confirmed in my sense of rightness when, as I was about to cross the Bay Bridge into San Francisco, I passed a field of "junk art." A figure sculpted out of pipes and other metal objects held a sign that, although it was meant for someone else, I took as a message from God for me. The sign read, WELCOME HOME, STELLA.

It seems paradoxical to say that pessimism is akin to hope, but in the same way it can also be true that hope is related to, and requires, hopelessness. It is only when the bottom drops out of our hopelessness, only when we have reached the end of the rope of hope and have been enveloped by the realization that all is lost, that we are positioned to experience the hope that is of God. This is the truth that T. S. Eliot refers to in "East Coker" when he says, "Be still and wait without hope. For hope would be hope for the wrong thing."[4] Hope for the "wrong thing" is hoping life will change, or hoping our attempts to muscle change will work. Hope for the right thing is relying on Mystery's muscle, whose strength is manifest through our efforts.

Hope is a term that points to the mystery of God's life in us. We are alive with a dynamism that is holy. Hope permeates all of life and moves us to find, in the words of psychiatrist Gerald May, "the courage and the fundamental human competence to taste the full flower of every particle of life and to respond with absolutely fierce, risking-trust to what is needed in every moment."[5] Hopefulness, far from being passive, propels us into every moment and every relationship. It enables us to give our all no matter what the odds. Hope that is based on the belief in or experience of God's faithful presence allows us to withstand disappointment and defeat, and to persevere beyond the limits of our strength. Hope is a lifeline to the grace of God within.

I would like to think that I am a hopeful person even though I no longer spend much time or energy wishing for things I don't have, or expecting that life will unfold in the way I want it to. Hope has become a matter of embracing life as it is, knowing that the communion with God I long for is a reality in the best and worst of times. The virtue (strength) of hope is grounded in the reality of the Ground of Being. It is this sacred presence from which I can draw "the strength to live and continually try new things" (as Kathy Coffey puts it in the text chosen for the second epigraph to this chapter), so that my world and the world around me might become what they truly are but have not yet been.

Meditations

True hope is not hoping for something I desire or hoping that it will come to pass. True hope is hoping in the reality of you, my God, present in the fabric of life. Hope involves the recognition that you are is the inscape of all that exists—even those aspects of reality (times, places, people, and events) that break our hearts. When this awareness leads me to embrace life as it is, my actions give witness to your presence that breathes in me, and my life becomes characterized by the qualities of positiveness, aliveness, confidence, and the willingness to take on new and challenging tasks.

When I am open to the hope that informs me, I experience the energy and vitality of Life. There is within us a sustaining force that cannot be defeated, one that by nature lives even when I despair. To give way to the feeling of hopelessness is to be unfaithful to the inner hope that is your aliveness in me. My resistance to the inclination to hopelessness is itself a sign of the persistent nature of hope. It is in us to "bounce back," to rejuvenate, to grow, and to become better, stronger, more compassionate, and wise through life's ups and downs. We can never lose hope, never shake its unrelenting presence, but we can lose touch with its power to recreate us.

The feeling of hope that I sometimes experience, though less often now than in my youth, is not true hope any more than infatuation is true love, though both are glimmers of the deeper reality whence they emerge. Hope is a virtue, not a feeling. It is a strength (virtus). Living a hopeful life, like living a loving life, is a matter of the will. It is a decision that must be made over and over again as we face situations that seem to be beyond our ability to endure. In fact, there is much that is beyond us, but there is nothing that we cannot find the strength to cope with when we draw upon your hopeful presence within.

❧ ❧

The hopefulness in which I live is embodied in all creation, for it too exists as a dimension of your life. Nature is hope-filled. The emergence and decay, the birth and death of plant and animal life, is Life unfolding in forms different from, yet related to, my own. The sometimes violent, sometimes calm vacillations that are nature's way reveal something of the way our lives unfold. We can learn the virtue of hope from other life-forms as they patiently comply with the seasons of the year and with the cycles of life. With this awareness, everything can be a source of wonder and can "re-member" us to the truth of the earth's sacredness and hope's enduring presence.

❧ Personal Reflections ❧

Chapter 9

Charity

What is charity? Charity is the virtue by which we love God above all things for His own sake, and our neighbor as ourselves for the love of God.

A CATECHISM OF CHRISTIAN DOCTRINE

One dark night, fired by love's urgent longing—ah the sheer grace! I went out unseen, my house being now all steeled.

ST. JOHN OF THE CROSS, *THE DARK NIGHT*

The bottom line of all the great religions of the world is love. The love of God, neighbor (whether friend or foe), and one's self is the defining characteristic of all people who are serious about their ultimate destiny and their relationship with the Divine.

A hymn often sung in Christian churches begins with the words "Where charity and love prevail there God is ever found." Although the hymn seems to imply that charity and love are two different things, I was always under the impression that they were one and the same. Love was charity, and charity was about being generous with my time and my toys. Love as charity made love more concrete and less sentimental, but it also reduced love, making it more a matter of helping and handouts rather than the gift of one's self. I recall hearing individuals and groups needing assistance with money, food, shelter, and the like referred to as "charity cases." Identifying those in need and responding to them was considered the heart and soul of love understood as charity.

I also recall hearing a threefold distinction made in reference to love: *eros* (erotic/romantic love), *filia* (familial love), and *agape* (universal/altruistic love). Though my friends and I knew that there was value in all of these, and that the latter was the highest form of love, it was always *eros* that took first place when we put it to a vote!

While speaking recently with a man who was unhappy with how he felt toward "problem people"—those with whom he was at odds—I was reminded of another concept about love I once held. This man said he wanted to love those who hurt him rather than harbor resentment against them. What he meant was that he wanted not only to return kindness for injury, to be charitable despite his anger, hurt, and disappointment, but to be able to *like* those who had offended him. This is certainly an admirable goal, but what it implies is that liking another person is an essential ingredient of loving him or her. This makes love a matter of feeling rather than willing—that is, deciding to value and respond to individuals based on the inherent goodness of their being, and independent of how we feel about them.

Like the man I just mentioned, I was taught that if I could manage to muster warmth for people (despite, in some cases, my inclination to the opposite), I could feel satisfied that I had hit the most important mark my religion required. I knew that I could exercise basic charity toward people I didn't like; that is, I could return good for evil and refuse to say anything to or about them that was unkind. (I can still hear someone—I'm not sure if it was a nun or my mother—instructing me: "If you can't say something nice about someone, don't say anything." I was quiet a lot!) But I had trouble with that next step: I never figured out how to like people I didn't like, and so when it came to dealing with those who hurt me, I always had a vague sense that I fell short of what true charity required.

Whether in the realm of feelings or actions, the command to love God and my neighbor was a struggle, because it required the defeat of self-love—which, despite the gospel injunction to love God and neighbor *as yourself*, was portrayed as the great barrier to love. In its worst forms, pride and vanity, this aberration of true love resulted in self-absorption, a trait which, I was correctly taught, could cause me to overlook my faults and be unaware of, and unresponsive to, others' needs.

It is surely true that love of one's self can become a fixation. Fueled by insecurity and the need to be considered attractive and popular, we can get to the point where we can hardly take our eyes off ourselves. In relation to appearance, this problem is most observable in teenagers, many of whom find it hard to pass a mirror or a window without staring at their reflection and judging their acceptability by the standards of the culture. Though we become skilled at hiding the tendency to look, many of us continue to be consumed, narcissistically or critically, by our appearance and our performance.

The fear of falling prey to pride and vanity rarely, if ever, prevented me from catching a glimpse of my reflection, but it did blind me to the importance of self-love at a deeper level. The necessity of self-love as a basis for emotional health and as a foundation for loving others is universally known today, but the impression left by my early religious training was that self-love and selfishness were too close for comfort. Paradoxically, my anxious efforts to keep self-love at bay resulted in self-absorption. I know now that less concern about pride and vanity would probably have made for more peace and sanity.

There is little doubt in my mind that without the awareness that love involves charity—concrete actions that address the immediate needs of others—my understanding of love would be sentimentally focused on feelings. And although I could have benefited from a healthier understanding of self-love, I feel fortunate to be sensitive to the fact that love turned inward has the capacity to blind me to my faults and to leave me absorbed with myself—oblivious to the needs of others.

Referring again to the analogy of inoculation, it can be said that many of us have been injected with love defined as charity and feeling, and have become resistant to the inner ache, the dis-ease, of the real thing. Both affect and action are important elements of love, but there is another dimension that is primary: longing. Love is more than feeling and more than charity, though it is expressed through our emotions and our deeds. Love is the center of our being, the core of our humanity. It is first and foremost about our spiritual anatomy, our communion with God.

Because we often walk through life without awareness that the love-bond with God is our essential self, we walk with a longing for completion that we seek to achieve through relationships, acquisitions, popularity, power, and the like. The great saints and mystics knew the cause and the fulfillment of our deepest desires. St. Augustine gave expression to this when he wrote: "For Thou hast made us for Thyself and our hearts are restless till they rest in Thee."[1] And John Donne states it poetically in his work "Batter My Heart":

Batter my heart three-personed God; for you
As yet but knock, breathe, shine, and seek to mend;
That I may rise and stand, o'erthrow me and bend
Your force to break, blow, burn and make me new. . . .
Take me to you, imprison me, for I,
Except you enthrall me, never shall be free,
Nor ever chaste, except you ravish me.[2]

The mystic in us knows the meaning of our restlessness and longing, for we are created with a yearning for a fullness that can never be satisfied apart from God. This very need is itself a dimension of the Divine. Love experienced as longing or desire is the heart of Love, the life of God within.

Even *eros*, the erotic longing we may feel for another person, is an expression of the deeper, vaster desire that is both for and from God. Every desire has its origin in Desire itself. Robert Farrar Capon put this notion in an earthy way when he wrote: "We turn each other on because we are made in the image of a God who is always on the make."[3] Even the physical/emotional rush we might experience in the presence of someone we may never see again is a hint of heaven, a piece of the passion that is God's longing for all creation.

The sacred attraction that influences our human nature is also found in Mother Nature. All things, from the order of celestial bodies to the forces at work in plant and animal life, participate in Love's longing and in the ultimate order of creation. *Ordo est amour:* "Order is love." Perhaps this is why so many people feel connected to God and experience one-ness with creation while observing a sunrise, standing at the ocean's edge, walking in a forest, or gazing upon a mountain range. The face of God can be seen in all that is. The power of God unites every aspect of life.

Through our attraction to others we incarnate the truth that God is "on the make." But the God-grounded longing we experience in our attraction to each other is only one way that our relationships disclose God-love. Another has to do with promoting the physical and spiritual well-being not only of those to whom we are drawn, but also those who rub us the wrong way. In responding to the needs of all others, we incarnate the truth that God is a healing presence that is attentive not only to some but to all. God is not only on the make, but "on the mend" as well.

Manifesting the full extent of God-love is not just a mat-ter of charity understood as giving to or helping others; it is about the willingness to lay down our lives for each other. There is a story about a chicken and a pig that illustrates this. The two were out for a stroll on a hot summer morning. After a long and tiresome time they came upon a restaurant with a sign that read "Ham and Eggs." The chicken said, "Let's go in; I'm starving." The pig responded adamantly, "Not me, pal. For you it's merely a question of involvement, but for me it's a matter of total commitment!"

I learned in my early church years that love was about involvement and that involvement was about give-and-take—but mostly give. If I gave someone what he or she needed, I could walk away like a chicken having laid an egg, or a rich person having put large sums into the Temple treasury (Luke

21:1), content that I had been loving even though my efforts had cost me nothing. But it is the pig in the story that represents both true love and our resistance to paying its price, because true love, whether it be for a person or an ideal, always involves a commitment, in good times and in bad, that both requires and results in the death of our selfish self—that dimension of us that's capable of placing our preferences before anyone and everyone else.

My niece has learned this lesson, as have many others, through parenting. She told me of the time someone asked her how she was taking care of herself now that she had two young children just over a year apart. Her response was: "It's not about me." Of course, it's important to take care of ourselves as we care for others, but love has a way of moving us beyond self-concern.

As we grow to realize that our longing for God calls us not only to help those who have been harmed, but to prevent harm from happening in the first place, we enter the arena of love that is justice. Justice is part of the dis-ease of love, because it challenges us to move beyond the tendency to equate love with feelings and charitable deeds, the tendency to have love characterize our relationships only with those who belong to our inner circle of family, friends, colleagues, fellow citizens, and the like. It is easy to fall prey to the notion that our responsibility to love not only begins but ends with those who like us or who are like us. Justice moves us to ask tough questions and take radical action. Marcus Borg writes with characteristic clarity about the difference between charity and justice:

> Charity and kind deeds are always good; there will always be need for help.

But the individualization of compassion means that one does not ask how many of the suffering are in fact victims. . . . Justice means asking why there are so many victims and then doing something about it.[4]

This distinction is illustrated by the story about two missionaries who left their compound to walk to a nearby river. As they stood watching the current, they saw a dead body floating downstream. They waded into the water, retrieved the body, dug a grave, and buried it. They then returned to the river and saw two more bodies. After burying them, they returned again and saw four bodies. It was then that one of them turned to the other and said, "Don't you think it's time we went upstream?"

Charity binds wounds and buries bodies. Justice seeks to remedy the cause of the problem, the source of the symptom. Because love is of God, and God is the spiritual ground of all people, true love is universal in scope and calls us to do what we can to abolish injustice and uphold the dignity of every person.

From a faith-perspective, the dignity of every person has to do with the truth that love is primarily the bond that unites us to the Divine within. The reality of our union with God is what makes selfishness so tragic and self-love so important. Selfishness is not a matter of attending to our own needs and desires; it is the limited understanding that we are our needs and desires. Selfishness is born of our ignorance of the holiness of ourselves; this issues in living for ourselves at the expense of others.

Self-love, on the other hand, is a way of thinking about and relating to ourselves and others that arises from an awareness of the Godness of every person. The fruit of this consciousness is seen when, despite her inability to be patient with the tirades of her Alzheimer's-afflicted husband, a caregiving wife refuses to berate herself. It is likewise evident when, in response to the costly error of an employee, the employer responds by pointing out the lessons to be learned rather than being critical and demeaning.

Love understood as charity (good deeds) is admirable, but limited. Love understood as emotion (positive feelings) is itself positive, but can be sentimental. Self-love that focuses on the fulfillment of our needs and desires is not innately wrong, but can become selfish. But when we realize that our spiritual longings are the fount of love, we come to understand that our deeds and feelings, our actions and affections, our selves and others are, in all their earthiness, a dimension of our relationship with God.

Meditations

*Love is your life in us O, God. When we care for another in feel-
ing and/or action, you are manifest through our person. I don't
please you when I love; I give expression, through loving, to you.
What I call love is a sacrament of Love, a concrete, human sign of
that which is always greater than the particular instance that is
an expression of it. Anything that is unloving—violence, indiffer-
ence, etc.—is a sacrilege, in that it keeps the Love that informs our
being from manifesting itself through our attitudes and actions.*

*A plant is drawn toward the sun for reasons that can be explained
scientifically. I am drawn to others for reasons that can be
explained psychologically. The force at work in both is Love, which
is embodied in the makeup of all creation. That which moves us
toward what we require in order to be fully alive is what is referred
to when we say, "God is Love." Your divinity is at the heart of reality, moving all creation to the wholeness that is holiness. God is a
name for the benevolence at work in nature and human nature,
that loving force that promotes life and holds all reality in a mutu-
ally sustaining state of existence and of becoming.*

*There is in all of creation a divine harmony and unity that,
along with the innate longing/yearning that compels us toward
what we require, is the reality of your love. My limited capacity*

to comprehend often results in my seeing and judging life by my own standards. I see what I consider to be good and bad, what is and what should be, myself and others, either and or. But life is more than meets the eye. In all the apparent opposites that comprise life in this world, there is a relationship of love understood as unity. Everything fits, whether I think/feel it does or not. My preference for how I want life to be blinds me to the harmonious truth that is the order in chaos. "There is a season for everything under heaven" (Eccles. 3:1).

"Charity begins at home," but it doesn't end there. The decision to live a life of love in relation to others is on shaky ground if I'm not able to take a loving stance toward myself. My inclination to be self-critical and unforgiving of my faults—even in the name of attaining perfection or holiness—is no virtue. Love of self is a radical affirmation that requires patience, acceptance, compassion, and forgiveness. When I allow myself to love myself as I am, I am positioned to grow beyond those aspects of myself that make self-love difficult. From this foundation, the house of love for others can, and must, be built, for love is dynamic and cannot be contained. When our love is limited to self-love or love of those who are a part of us, it is not love in the broadest sense, and we are not all we are meant to be.

Personal Reflections

Chapter 10

Prayer

What is prayer? Prayer is the lifting up of our minds and hearts to God.

A CATECHISM OF CHRISTIAN DOCTRINE

To pray is to be in touch with oneself in a new way: to listen to the melody, not made by ourselves, that sounds at the core of our being and, from beyond the sickness that deafens us, summons us to be alive.

GREGORY BAUM, *MAN BECOMING*

Some years ago I served as a retreat director for a man who felt the need to focus on his relationship with God. On the last day of the five-day retreat he announced that he wanted to talk about prayer. He began by saying, "I'm in my mid-fifties. I'm a physician, a husband, and a father. I've grown intellectually, socially, emotionally, and professionally over the years, but I still pray the same way I did when I was in the second grade."

There's a touching simplicity to the prayer of a second-grader—we would be fortunate if that simplicity characterized our prayer for a lifetime. But childlike trust is only one dimension of prayer. Form, content, and purpose are another matter; they ought to reflect the growth and maturity we strive for in all aspects of our lives.

When I was in the second grade I said my prayers and read my prayers as I'd been taught. Prayer consisted of thanking, praising, pleading, and commending to God those I loved. My prayer sounded a lot like the following letters to God:

Dear God,
    Thank you for the baby brother, but what I prayed for was a puppy.[1]

                                                    Joyce

Dear God,
    Please put another holiday between Christmas and Easter. There is not anything good in there now.[2]

                                                    Ginny

The prayer of my youth was a one-way street, a way of letting God know how I felt and what I wanted. I was taught that if I prayed long enough and hard enough—in other words if I prayed right—God would love me, and what I hoped and asked for would come about—no matter how outragious the request:

Dear God,
    My brother is a rat. You should give him a tail. Ha Ha.[3]

                                                    Danny

Eventually my prayer grew beyond the second-grade level, at least in form. I learned new ways of praying—devotional practices like the rosary and ejaculations aimed at gaining indulgences. When I told a Protestant friend that I used to recite prayers called *ejaculations*, her response was classic. It was, to use computer imagery, as if the cursor in her brain had moved to the "B" in her mind's "tool bar" as she said, in bold letters, "**Ejaculations—you've got to be kidding!**" Those prayers, I explained to her, are one-liners such as "My Jesus, mercy" and "Mother of mercy, pray for us." Each such prayer earned three hundred days' indulgence, according to the Catechism (an indulgence being, according to that same source, "the remission granted by the Church of the temporal punishment due to sins already forgiven").[4] My arsenal of prayers increased as time went on, but my motive for praying remained unchanged: it was an attempt to get God's ear and to steer things in the direction I wanted them to go.

Given the ease with which I strayed from the "straight and narrow," I viewed prayer as a way to stay on the right path. If an idle mind was the devil's workshop, then a head full of prayers was a way of staving off temptation. This kind of prayer came in handy for everything from staying faithful to my Lenten resolution to swear off candy, to refraining from swearing of another sort. This prayer was done with furrowed brow and clenched jaw; it was more a matter of desperation than inspiration.

Along with private prayer, the Eucharist was a form of prayer that was a part of my early religious formation. Attending mass left me with a warm feeling of God's closeness and of being caught up in something larger than myself. But there was a strong sense of obligation attached to this prayer, and like the saying of private prayers, it was for me a way of pleasing and appeasing the God whose will it was that I attend mass every Sunday. I had no appreciation for the Eucharist as the prayer of the faith-community; it was merely another way, albeit a special one, to spend time with God. Though it was a public prayer, I entered into it as privately as if I were alone.

I found the prayer of my earlier years and childlike mentality very comforting. God was someone I went to with my needs and fears, my hopes and hopelessness. I didn't always get what I prayed for, but I felt a bond with God and appreciated the security of knowing there was a "port in the storm." The prayer of my youth served to establish in me the conviction that whatever imagined distance or barrier might have separated me from God—a very real sense much of the time—I could be in relationship with what was ultimate. I was not alone, nor was I without recourse when life seemed overwhelming.

As I've grown spiritually, I have ceased to find much meaning or comfort in rote prayer. Because I've changed, my way of praying has also changed. I believe that it was the Spirit in the retreatant I mentioned that fueled his desire to mature in prayer. It was his God-self that knew there had to be another and more satisfying way of relating to God. As in any developing relationship of a romantic nature, when love becomes more urgent, words cease to be enough. As our sense of God becomes more personal and intimate, saying prayers becomes less fulfilling. Even trading formula prayers for the spontaneity of our own words—a definite step beyond the second grade—can feel inadequate.

It may be that when formula prayers and devotional

practices become dry and lifeless, we are being invited to a type of prayer that is more intimate and wordless, one that is less about communication and more about communion. Here we are asked to forget not only our needs and concerns, but our very self. Here we are at home in the comfort and security of a Presence that both holds and enfolds us. Just a quiet being with God can be sufficient—resting, waiting, and listening with the "ear of the heart." Nothing has to be said or felt, and nothing has to happen. The point is to just be in the Presence that is God. It's simple, but most of us find it profoundly difficult to let this be enough, because we've learned that prayer is something we *do*, and when it's done there should be some tangible result, like a feeling of peace or a world-changing insight. But this type of prayer is in keeping with the Buddhist dictum "Don't just do something; stand there," as well as with the summons expressed in Psalm 46:10, "Be still and know that I am God."

While on retreat at Genesee Abbey some years ago, I came to a new understanding of prayer that made sense to the mystic in me. I was reading Matthew 26, where Jesus goes off to pray and asks his disciples to "stay awake." I was struck by the thought that perhaps it is not we who pray, but God. God's prayer is creation; it is what *is*—nature, people, and the events of our lives. All of this is the *Logos*, the Word, the prayer of God manifest as life. Like that of the disciples, our task, our part in this prayer, is to stay awake, to be present to the familiar tasks and ordinary events of life so as not to miss the sacred wonder of it all. Unfortunately, like them, we are too often asleep, too often oblivious to the utterances of the Divine that surround us and are us. We are present to God's prayer when we see that life is sacred and when we hear the holiness that resonates through every sound and event. Presbyterian minister Frederick Buechner writes about this:

> The swallow, the rooster, the workmen, my stomach, all with their elusive rhythms, their harmonies and disharmonies and counterpoint, became, as I listened, the sound of my own life speaking to me. . . . [T]hat is what I mean by saying that God speaks into or out of the thick of our days.
>
> He speaks not just through the sounds we hear, of course, but through events in all their complexity and variety.[5]

Because God is the Ground of all that is, and because all creation is holy, we are immersed in God's prayer by virtue of being alive. We exist in relationship to God not as people who communicate with the Divine, but as enfleshed expressions of the One with whom we are one. The intimacy of this relationship is the deepest meaning of prayer. It is this ongoing abiding in God that we become present to when we enter into life's joys and sorrows with a heart and mind open to their sacredness. Prayer thus understood is an acknowledgment that although we are just passing through this world, it is our home away from home.

Too many to count are the number of people I have heard say that they cannot pray when they are angry, grief-stricken, or otherwise upset. Continued conversation with them inevitably discloses that by *pray* they mean *speak polite words to God*, and/or *feel God's consoling presence*. Many of us have learned that when we pray we should be on our best behavior; no wonder, then, that we find it difficult to pray when what we feel is less than best (and sometimes downright ugly).

But if prayer is a dimension of our relationship with God, and if healthy relationships require honesty, then we must be willing to own and express to God who and how we are, whether or not we like what we think and feel. The groan that emanates from a broken heart and the fist that pounds a table in rage can be wordless prayers that unite us to God, who is one with us in our emotional valleys as well as on our peaks.

Along with opening to life and emotional honesty, another aspect of mature prayer has to do with the willingness to listen and respond to what God "speaks" in us. I once had a person in spiritual direction tell me that he was afraid to listen to God in prayer because he was sure he would be told to let go of the things he loved most. In particular, he feared he would have to give up golf! I hope God has bigger concerns, but I know that when we hold willfully to anyone or anything in life, God can appear to oppose us. I find it amazing that God doesn't grow weary of the foolish machinations by which we make God into an ogre—at least I hope she doesn't! But I believe that, if we remain still enough and quiet enough for long enough, we may experience the divine summons calling us not only to rest in God, but also to leave our comfort zones.

Those who have grown to appreciate and to prefer quiet prayer to thinking, speaking, or reading words addressed to God do not cease to give praise or thanks or to petition God, asking for what we desire. But as we mature in the spiritual life, we come to realize that we do not pray *to* God, we pray *from* God. In prayer we give voice to the sacred depths of ourselves, whence comes the longing for health of mind and body, peace in the world, harmony in relationships, safety for ourselves and those we love, and all the many things we desire. Our prayer is, in the words of St. Paul, the groaning of the Spirit within us (Rom. 8:23).

When we pray from the awareness of our communion with God, we are less likely to ask for what we think will make us happy, and more likely to pray for the courage to surrender to God's ways, to follow that circuitous path that strips us of our ego and reveals the folly of what we think should take place. When we are open to the wisdom of God manifest in life's unfolding, we can affirm the truth posed in answer to the question, "Do you know how to make God laugh? Tell her your plans!"

In any case, the notion of answers to prayer has taken on a new meaning for me. Robert Farrar Capon says that there are three answers to prayer: "Yes, no," and *"we'll* see"![6] The latter doesn't mean that God, looking pensive and stroking his beard, says, "Let me think about that." "We'll see" is a response of solidarity; it means that God walks the path of our life with us. God shares in the joys and sorrows, the confusion and clarity, the desperation and inspiration that form the yin and yang of existence, because our being is a participation in God's Being. I have come to realize that prayer is always answered—in fact, it's answered before it's even thought or spoken!—and that the answer is the Presence that accompanies us all the days of our life.

Even though God is closer to us than we are to ourselves, and despite the fact that God knows our needs and desires before they are spoken, it is important to give expression to our thoughts and feelings in prayer, because our life is a partnership with the Divine. Partners communicate verbally and otherwise as they maneuver through life. They make adjustments, fine-tuning themselves according to the needs of the other and the good of their relationship. So too with regard to God: we entrust ourselves by communicating what matters most to us, and in this vulnerability, this willingness to be totally honest, we are involved in the ongoing re-creation of the dynamic partnership with God that is our personal share in the larger mystery that is the dance of humanity and Divinity.

I have come to value liturgical prayer more as I grow in awareness and appreciation of the communion of humanity and Divinity and the bond that all people share, given our common spiritual essence. It makes sense to me to gather with others to give praise to and for the mystery of it all—the divine depths, the sacred iceberg of which creation is the tip. What was once a public event at which I maintained a private communication with God has become for me a communal celebration of the faith-community's beliefs during which I am conscious of God's real presence incarnate in my fellow worshipers. Liturgy can be a powerful experience, one that re-members its participants to one another and to that which they hold sacred.

Except in the context of liturgy, I am no longer drawn to the recitation of formula prayers. Although I have ceased to ask God for favors, I still give expression, in word and thought, to my deepest needs and longings as a means of anchoring petitionary prayer in the everyday reality of my life. But the most meaningful way for me to pray is a matter of awareness. Whether sitting still in meditative silence or being about the tasks of the day, I attempt, with limited success, to be present, staying awake to the sacred center of every moment, person, and event.

Meditations

"You pray best when you don't know you are praying" is a statement attributed to one of the Desert Fathers. I had always thought that if I didn't know I was praying when I was saying my prayers, I must be distracted. Thus the prayer of my youth was very self-conscious and intentional. I realize now that if I know I'm praying (meditating), there's too much of me involved. If prayer is an experience of communion with you, the less conscious I am of myself the better. Likewise, the less conscious of you (imagined as a separate being) I am, the better. For prayer is a matter of being in you, who are the reality of myself. Prayer is primarily a state of being awake, not of feeling or consciousness.

When we are in the presence of someone who loves us, we are at home. We are free to be who and how we happen to be at the time—grouchy or pleasant, mad or sad. When we sit in stillness with the intent of communing with you, we sit in freedom and in the embrace of total acceptance. But this does not necessarily mean that nothing is asked of us. Often, in the quiet, we sense that there is something we must do in order to be true to ourselves. It is sometimes experienced as a whisper and sometimes as a shout. It can be a gentle nudge or a not so subtle shove. In prayer we encounter you as very real and often very active. Your Spirit comforts the afflicted and afflicts the comfortable.

But it can also be the case that we encounter silence, emptiness, and darkness in prayer. Your "absence" can feel as real as your presence. I am tempted, in the face of the lack of feeling, to grasp for what I cannot feel or to presume that something I am doing or not doing is the cause of this sense of no sense of you. The point of prayer is not to feel your warmth or to experience the guiding action of your Spirit. The point of prayer is to affirm, in quiet stillness, the truth that my being and all of life is infused with you (felt or not). To pray thus is to affirm that though I may feel lost, I am at home. Though I may feel restless, there is nowhere I need to go. Though I feel at a distance from you and want to bridge the gap, I can do nothing to achieve this union, for it "was in the beginning, is now, and ever shall be."

Prayer requires silence within, a cessation of thinking in order to rest in the completeness of the mystery that is my being in you. This inner stillness is a celebration of the truth that you abide me. Prayer is not primarily a matter of communication but of communion. It is being in a state of intimacy—one with what informs me. Praying is like breathing; it is a participation in that in which I am immersed and which sustains me. Just as breathing occurs in me without intention, so am I unconsciously and continually in prayerful communion with your pervasive Presence.

Personal Reflections

Chapter 11

Sacraments

What is a sacrament? A sacrament is an out-
ward sign instituted by Christ to give grace.
A CATECHISM OF CHRISTIAN DOCTRINE

This is a sacramental world. . . . [T]he range
of possible "sacraments" is very great. . . . [T]he
divine action is not confined to the ecclesiasti-
cally recognized channels.
JOHN MACQUARRIE, *PRINCIPLES OF*
CHRISTIAN THEOLOGY

The seven sacraments of the Catholic Church (Baptism, Confirmation, Holy Eucharist, Penance, Extreme Unction, Holy Orders, Matrimony) were, I learned in my early religious training, those events where heaven touched earth, where God reached across the chasm that separated humanity and Divinity and conferred something of the sacred. Sacraments were sacred moments for me—times when time stood still and I entered into the cloud of God's immutable presence.

When I was a child, sacraments seemed magical to me in several ways. First, they were magical in the same way that going to Briggs Stadium to watch the Detroit Tigers play baseball was magical. There was an atmosphere that was both unique and charged. At the stadium, the smell of cigar smoke, the taste of mustard-smeared hotdogs, the stunning sight of the vast expanse of brilliant green grass, the energy of the crowd, and the presence of my heroes on the field all contributed to the magic. I was in another world, a sacred place, one I hated to leave.

While the magical drama of big-league baseball games is always played out in a stadium, the magic of sacraments unfolds in the confines of a church. St. Francis de Sales Church was the "stadium," the venue, for the sacraments of my youth. Its magical atmosphere consisted of hard wooden pews with soft-cushioned kneelers, hymns sung by choirs, prayers spoken in Latin, the odor of incense, stained-glass windows, statues, and an aura of God's presence that was as tangible as it was invisible.

Besides the aura or atmosphere of churches, the other way in which sacraments struck me as magical was in the literal "hocus pocus" or "the hand is quicker than the eye" sense. It was by means of a word and/or gesture that bread and wine became, on the spot, Christ's body and blood in the Eucharist. The term "hocus pocus" is said to have originated from the Latin words *Hoc est enim corpus meum* ("This is my body"), which were spoken over the bread during mass. In the same way, the stain of "original sin" was washed away in Baptism, one's sins were forgiven in the confessional, the Holy Spirit was conferred in Confirmation, couples were married at their wedding, men became priests at ordination ceremonies, and those at the point of death were given, in the sacrament of Extreme Unction (now called the Sacrament of the Sick), grace and remission of their sins. In the twinkling of an eye something that was, was no longer, or something that was not became a reality. David Copperfield had nothing on the priest through whom sacramental sleight of hand happened.

"Sacramentals" are close relatives of sacraments. These are holy objects such as statues, and actions such as blessings, that are used to gain spiritual and temporal favors; for example, bodily health, material blessings, and protection from evil spirits. Though intended to aid one's awareness of, and connection to, God, sacramentals often took on the same magical character as sacraments. The burning of palms to protect against lightning strikes and the burying of a statue of St. Joseph upside down to hasten the selling of a house are examples of how sacramentals became confused with superstition, how objects of devotion were imbued with magical powers they did not possess.

As an adolescent I was always impressed by the piety of professional athletes who made the sign of the cross (a sacramental intended to remind the faithful that they were claimed by Christ) when at bat in a baseball game, or before launching a basketball foul shot. I wasn't sure what to make of it when, despite this gesture (which I interpreted as recruiting God to their side), the player struck out or bounced the ball off the rim. Perhaps, I reasoned, God had bigger fish to fry.

I am as skeptical of magic as an adult as I was entranced by it when I was a child. I know now what I didn't know in my youth—namely, that acts of magic are a matter of illusion and appearance, and that magical places, though real, are given their power by those who behold them. Though my impression of the Catholic Church's sacraments in my childhood may have been magical/superstitious (and therefore misleading), participation in them gave me the conviction that has formed my current thinking about what they celebrate—namely, that life is more than meets the eye, and that the power that is God is at work in nature and human nature.

I no longer believe that sacraments are magic, nor do I, for the most part, experience a rush when I enter a church. Though I know and honor the unique nature of the sacraments of all Christian religions, I now realize that there are "seventy times seven" ways in which the invisible mystery we call God is manifest in life.

I have come to understand the sacraments not as magic but as mystery. They are not illusions; they are illuminating—that is, they shed light on the often dimly lit reality of the God-filled nature of life, relationships, and everyday events. When we celebrate a sacrament, we don't make something happen; we make something of the truth that what's happening within us, around us, and to us is holy. The movement of a ballet dancer embodies the gracefulness of God. The voices of a choir resonate with holy harmony. Sunrises and sunsets are an epiphany of a sacred beauty. The response to another's need, be it with one's time, money, or expertise, is an incarnation of Divinity's generosity and compassion.

I have asked myself many times why and how I have come to believe what I believe about the sacramental character of life. I cannot say when it happened that the once firmly drawn line between sacred and secular began to blur, but blur it has. Not long ago that fact was made clear to me while I was making a retreat at Genesee Abbey. I was walking the road between Nazareth, the house assigned to retreatants staying for an extended period—two months, in my case—and the buildings that compose the monastery proper. As I looked at one of the buildings, I had a sense, not a thought, that it was more than it appeared to be. I experienced the same sense about the trees my gaze fell upon. The same was true for every person I encountered all that day, and for myself as well. Everything and everyone and every action was more than it appeared to be. To this day I cannot explain why this happened, precisely what it felt like, or what it meant, but I do know that it was a subtle experience of transfiguration, a seeing into the sacred, sacramental depth of creation.

All of life is a sacrament manifesting that which is essentially transcendent, and each one of us is baptized (initiated), confirmed (strengthened), and ordained (blessed) to carry out the task of making real that which is ideal—bringing to light and to life the latent holiness that infuses creation. By our real presence (a theological term generally used to indicate Jesus' actual presence in the bread and wine) we are all receivers and givers of Eucharist; that is, we are fed and feed others physically, emotionally, and spiritually as we journey through life. A divine mercy is granted to us and through us a thousand times over as we forgive and are forgiven for offenses intended and unintended: "For those whose sins you forgive, they are forgiven . . ." (John 20:23). We are all wedded to one another, and by honoring each other for better and for worse we disclose God's covenanted love. And when we enter into each other's infirmities, we anoint one another with a God-presence that can heal the soul if not the body.

If it isn't clear by now, I'll make it so: in its broadest sense, the sacrament of God's presence and power is not limited to places designated as holy, nor is it conveyed exclusively by those who are ordained. The entire world is a cathedral wherein Divinity is disclosed. Where we work as well as where we worship, where we play as well as where we pray—that is the venue of the Holy. And every person is a temple of, and a vehicle for, God's self-communication, no matter how successful we've been at making a mess of our lives.

God lives here in our less-than-perfect, full-of-flaws selves. The sacrament of God's real presence may be neat and clean in the bread and wine of the Eucharist, but it is a messy mystery in human beings. It may smell like incense and sound like a harmonious choir in church, but body odors and dissonant lives, though less compelling, are no less holy epiphanies of the incarnate reality of God.

Some time ago, while giving the eucharistic bread to a woman during mass, I was delightfully surprised by her response to my statement "The body of Christ." The prescribed response is "Amen," but some people say, "Yes," "So be it," "It is," or other such statements that make sense to them. The woman I'm speaking of replied, "We are." Speaking not only for herself, but for all present (and perhaps for all Christians), she affirmed the truth that the body of Christ is not a piece of bread; it is primarily people who nourish themselves with it and who attempt to live in a way that honors what that bread is a sign of—the real presence of Christ in humanity.

From the understanding that the sacrament of God's presence is not limited to certain places and some people, it follows that sacraments should not be equated with cere-monies. A ceremony celebrates and proclaims an already existing and/or ongoing reality. The sacrament that is cele-brated and proclaimed is the living out of our lives and rela-tionships in such a way that God is disclosed through them. It is in the quiet, gradual blending of their lives that two people, long before their wedding, reveal that Divinity is wed-ded to humanity for better and for worse. It is in forgiving one another that we demonstrate the undefeated mercy of God. And so with all the "official" sacraments, they are the cultic display of the everyday, incarnate reality of the holiness of life and relationships happening. They are the ritual enactment of the real presence of God's action in the world. They are mythic and mysterious and, therefore, much more powerful and empowering than magic.

In saying this, I do not mean to imply that the ceremonies at which sacraments are celebrated are without meaning or power; in fact, the opposite is true. Sacramental ceremonies have the ability to bring about in us a deepening realization of the abiding presence of the Divine. And although participating in them is not, as I was once taught, necessary for salvation, engagement in these ritual events can root us in the saving truth that we are always and everywhere in God.

The disclosure of the Divine is both constant and unlimited. It is more fleshy than flashy, more ordinary than extraordinary—which is why we often miss it. But whether God is seen or unseen, the fact remains that everything and everyone is an "outward sign" of this inward truth.

When we begin to see the world as sacramental, every piece of it is recognized as *a sacramental.* This truth is well put by singer/songwriter Peter Mayer in this verse from his song "Holy Now":

This morning outside I stood
And saw a little red-winged bird
Shining like a burning bush
And singing like a scripture verse
It made me want to bow my head
I remember when church let out

How things have changed since then
Everything is holy now[1]

All creation is holy and is capable of awakening us to God. Every object, person, and event has the potential to be a "thin place" where God's self-communication is experienced. With every word and gesture we preside at the liturgy of our lives, wherein the Divine is brought to light and to life in and through us.

I find sacramental celebrations to be powerful experiences that renew my awareness of and relationship with God and with the community of believers. But I no longer have an understanding of sacraments that limits them to ceremonial words and gestures. Seeing life with the eyes of faith has revealed the sacramental nature of creation itself. What is ritualized in church is actualized in life.

Meditations

Although the ceremonies that celebrate them may be elaborate, there is nothing fancy about sacraments. They come to us in the ordinariness of our lives: our every encounter with nature is simply sacred, and our interactions with other people bring us face to face with your unadorned holiness. When we realize, with our hearts as well as our minds, that the essence of us is your divinity enfleshed, our imperfect bodies, our taken-for-granted relationships, our everyday lives are recognized for what they are—your dance in time and space. Everything from the beating of our hearts to the preparation of a meal is a kind of liturgy wherein the sacred expresses itself without pretentiousness.

The elements of a sacrament—the bread and wine used at the Eucharist, for example—are more than meets the eye even before ritual prayers are spoken over them. So it is with all of life. Whether we see it or not and whether we express it in words or remain silent, every dimension of life is imbued with your holiness and gives expression to it. Independent of our awareness, our words, and our actions, creation is permeated with Divinity. When something is blest it is not made holy; rather, its inherent holiness is celebrated.

The neat and orderly celebration of sacraments can give the false impression that your presence that is ritualized in church but exists everywhere is also neat and orderly. However, the reality of your essential communion with creation is revealed in earthquakes as well as sunsets, in floods and hurricanes as well as the majesty of oceans and mountains, in the valleys as well as the peaks of our emotional lives. Every aspect of life embodies a dimension of the multifaceted Mystery that is your presence in our midst. We confine your boundless Spirit when we define as holy only certain places and specific people. You are in the secular as well as the sacred, in the sinner as well as the saint.

Like time purposely set aside for personal prayer, ceremonial sacraments take place at specific times and in designated places. We "go there" to enter into a mythic enactment, a timeless truth that unfolds in time. Although the truth celebrated in ritualized sacraments is boundless, the ambience created by our gathering and by the sights, sounds, and smells of the liturgy is charged with the Holy and has the power to transform us and transport us to a felt experience of what we celebrate. There is a soulfulness to liturgy that, for all its concreteness, points to another dimension of life. Liturgy is the proverbial "finger pointing to the moon"; it is a means to an end. But the condition of the finger, the beauty of the liturgy, though it can distract us from the truth it celebrates, can also give us a taste of it that whets our appetite for more.

❧ *Personal Reflections* ❧

Chapter 12

Morality

Besides believing what God has revealed, what else must we do to be saved? Besides believing what God has revealed, we must keep His law.

A CATECHISM OF CHRISTIAN DOCTRINE

Surely, this commandment . . . is not too hard for you, nor is it too far away. . . . [I]t is in your mouth and in your heart.

DEUTERONOMY 30:11, 14

Along with the body of beliefs and requirements of worship, morality—the dictates governing behavior—constitutes the heart of religious practice. Nutshell notions such as the "golden rule" (sometimes interpreted as "Those who have the gold rule"!) express the gist of moral teachings, but the quintessential delineation of morality in the Judeo-Christian tradition is found in the Decalogue, the Ten Commandments.

The commandments were given to Moses and the Israelites as a sign of Yahweh's favor and to assist them in living up to their end of the covenant—to be God's people. It didn't take long for the commandments, and the six hundred–plus precepts of the law that became associated with them, to become burdensome—a sign of God's demandingness.

In the time of Jesus, some pharisaical sects were exacting and unrelenting in their observance of the law, and they demanded perfection of others in its exercise. There was no corner of life that was devoid of prescriptions that kept the people focused on doing the right thing in the right way at the right time. Despite Jesus' condemnation of pharisaical legalism, most Christian churches have come to embody it, and to preach and teach that the commandments, rather than being love's parameters, are God's criteria for judgment.

For anyone growing up in a mainline religious tradition, the words "Thou shalt not" have a familiar and fearsome ring. In my experience the restrictive dimension of the commandments and other moral dictates received more emphasis than did the teachings of love they were supposed to give flesh to. These rubrics of behavior promoted a self-consciousness that robbed life of spontaneity. Like the constant refrain of negatives that so easily spill forth from the lips of well-meaning parents—"Don't touch that," "Don't open that," "Don't eat that"—a morality expressed primarily in the negative can create a hesitancy and restrictiveness that impedes rather than promotes true moral development.

Keeping the commandments was, in my mind, the measure of my relationship with God. They were the checklist that indicated whether I was in the fast lane to heaven or on the slippery slope to that other destination. The emphasis that was given to obeying the commandments was consistent with the understanding that being a good Christian amounted to being a good boy or girl.

The reality of morality that I encountered in my youth was fear- and reward-based. It focused on individual righteousness and encouraged a confining carefulness. It emphasized not doing harm and not making waves. It was about drawing inside the lines and not living outside the box. Fear of punishment and hope for reward, though the least mature motivation for moral behavior, was and still remains the most prevalent one among churchgoing/"God-fearing" people. Those who taught me right from wrong did so with my best interests in mind: "We'll get him to heaven by scaring the hell out of him!"

I recall going home following my Monday afternoon Catechism class one day and telling my mother, "The nun said we would go to hell if we didn't keep the commandments." My mother did her best to counter that message, but it seemed to me, even at the tender age of seven, that in matters of morality, aprons carried less authority than religious habits.

Morality, as I learned it, was about living in the light. It was about doing good and avoiding evil, doing what was right always and what was wrong never, turning from sin and embracing virtue, keeping not only the spirit of the law, but its letter as well. I knew there were people who managed to pull this off, but I had no idea how. I never knew, until I heard the amusing story that follows, why I always felt hemmed in by rules, and wired to fail at my attempts to keep within their boundaries. I now realize that my Italian ancestry may have had something to do with it.

An American attorney was sent to do an assessment of the legal systems of four countries: Great Britain, Germany, Russia, and Italy. He reported that in Great Britain everything was permitted that was not prohibited. In Germany everything was prohibited that was not permitted. In Russia everything was prohibited, even that which was permitted. And in Italy everything was permitted, *especially* that which was prohibited!

When I was young my tendency to "push the envelope" felt rebellious, but that tendency was, and it remains, the prompting of a deeper morality of the heart—a prompting that calls all of us to challenge convention by what we say and how we live.

Although it was taught and imposed with a harshness that clouded its true purpose, my initial understanding of morality brought about in me an awareness of the fact that how I live my life has an impact, for better or worse, on myself and others. In the climate in which I learned them, the commandments called me to conformity more than to authenticity, but they instilled in me the same thing that is accomplished by the boundary-setting that loving parents impose upon their children: a sense of being valued and of being watched over. God's love was not sentimental but practical. I was given direction in life, and what I did or failed to do in response to that direction mattered.

Although I rebelled against rules and regulations in my youth, I now know the wisdom and necessity of having such guidelines, for without them I would, like a river without banks, tend to lose my direction, power, and sense of myself as someone with purpose. Paradoxically, we must be confined in order to be defined. We must be limited by love's dictates if we are to become who we are called to be— people free to love deeply and without limits.

Most people experience this paradox in the commitment of marriage. Phrases like "tying the knot" and "getting hitched," though spoken in jest, hint at the confining nature of marriage. Each party proclaims that the other will, for a lifetime, be their most significant other, no matter what. It is in the willingness to honor their vows by sharing their joys, abiding their sorrows, and working through their difficulties that each person grows as an individual and that both grow together as a couple. The practical demands of time and the emotional demands for attention are restrictive, in that there is only so much time in a day and only so much energy to expend. But the depth of love that can result through time and attention given could never be achieved without the parameters inherent in a committed relationship.

The moral behavior of a spiritually mature person is not motivated by feelings of guilt, fear, or the desire for reward. Neither is it focused exclusively on the self or on what should not be done. Rather, it is fueled by the awareness of God's communion with humanity and our oneness with one another. God, my neighbor, and myself are three dimensions of one holy Mystery. This is one reason that the commandments, all ten of them, need to be embraced. They are an articulation of a way of being that arises from love and that issues in loving relationships. Because God is incarnate in all people, morality calls us beyond concern for the state of our own soul and invites us to be proactive on behalf of others. It challenges us to speak for those who have no voice in our society, to be advocates for the marginalized. I have seen no stronger statement in reference to this understanding of morality than the one that hangs framed in the living room of some friends of mine: "If when they come to take the little ones they do so without having to step over your body, shame on your religion and your life."

Although it had probably been germinating for some time, my awareness that morality had something to do with social justice came to birth in me when I began graduate studies in theology in 1967. My professors were talking about the "social gospel," a way of reading the accounts of Jesus' life that focused on the political/social situation in which he lived, and his prophetic response to it. As I was absorbing this message, the political/social upheaval occasioned by the war in Vietnam and by the civil rights movement was in full swing. It became clear to me that my understanding of morality as primarily having to do with issues of purity and concern for my eternal destiny was narrow at best. I began to feel shame about my religion and my life, and I became more involved in the issues of the day.

The purpose of morality is not to help us gain an eternal reward or avoid everlasting punishment; rather, it is to promote responsibility, integrity, and a sense of justice. Because this is so, keeping the letter of the law is less important than honoring its spirit and being open to its power to transform us. A student, it is said, went to the rabbi and with great excitement proclaimed, "Rabbi, I have gone through the Torah." The rabbi, looking bored, returned to his reading. Again the student said, "Rabbi, I have gone through the Torah." Still the rabbi seemed uninterested. A third time the student stated, "Rabbi, I have—" The rabbi interrupted and said, "Yes, I know; you have gone through the Torah. But has the Torah gone through you?"

The Torah, the first five books of the Hebrew scriptures, is often referred to as "the law," though it also contains stories about Israel's origins. The rabbi in the above story knows that morality cannot be legislated. We don't live a moral life by keeping the commandments or other rules of behavior. We become moral people when the wisdom inherent in moral teachings transforms us into virtuous people, people who recognize the sacredness of humanity and who relate to ourselves and others with reverence and compassion, as Marcus Borg indicates: "The Christian life . . . is ultimately not about believing or about being good. Rather . . . it is about a relationship with God that involves us on a journey of transformation."[1]

Although I would like to think otherwise, I know that I need the parameters of law, rule, and commandment in order to live a truly moral life. But I now recognize that these dictates are not merely external impositions meant to steer me in the right direction. Their formulation, and the wisdom of adhering to them, is rooted in the fact that they give expression to the innate truth that God's law is written upon our hearts.

One of the Latin words for commandment is *imperito*, from which we take our word *imperative*. An imperative is an inner necessity. It is imperative that we breathe, for example. No one or no law—except that of our nature—need tell us to breathe; we do it (or, better said, it occurs in us) because we are human. Likewise, we are to act lovingly, which is the essence of the law, because it is our true nature to do so. God's law is written on our hearts. Living a moral life is less a matter of conformance to an externally imposed law than it is openness to the compelling presence of God's indwelling. Rules of conduct are like a conductor's directives to an orchestra—a means of bringing out the best that each and all have to offer, a help in making the individual contribution of each person part of a harmonious whole.

Morality is about doing right and living in the light, but every person has at least a touch of darkness within. We are all capable of words and deeds that are less than upstanding. To live in denial of this truth by striving for moral perfection can result in the opposite of what we strive for. As my spiritual director says, when we live too much in the light, we cast a long shadow.

I witnessed the truth of this statement in a man who had recently become a Christian. He was a good person who worked hard at becoming a better one. He was a devoted husband and father who, on business trips, found himself watching X-rated movies. This tendency both confused and frustrated him until he realized that he was probably trying too hard to be pure. When he became more relaxed with his sexual desires and fantasies, he lost interest in anything and everything pornographic. Moral teachings are important not only because they are an expression of the true self, but also because the power of denied darkness can undermine our best intentions.

The brand of morality that characterized my youth was moralism, a heavy-handed, self-righteous, religiously rigid focus on the letter of the law. The commandments were not imperatives I strove to embody; they were rules I was afraid to break. I didn't become a mature spiritual person by following them, but one who was preoccupied with perfection. I now view morality as a way of living that is consistent with my God-self—in other words, that embraces both my darkness and my light and is responsive to the needs of others. The power and importance of the commandments arises from the fact that they give expression to the truth by which we must live in order to be our best selves individually and collectively. Because God is embodied in our bodies, we must live in a way that honors the holiness of all people and of life itself.

Meditations

"Do not imagine that I have come to abolish the Law or the Prophets. I have come not to abolish but to complete them" (Matt. 5:17). Jesus completes the law (love) by being an embodiment of it. He lived a loving life, one characterized by compassion for the afflicted and inclusivity in relation to the marginalized. Morality is not a matter of conformity to God-given rules of behavior; it is about being true to our God-filled nature. The law that is your law is one that issues from within. I am faithful to the truth of who I am in you when I live in obedience to the law. It is my nature to love, though it is also in me to live at odds with love. The commandments tell me how I ought to live given my true identity; they show me what it looks like to function as the enfleshment of you that I am.

Morality has to do with a relationship of love for you, my neighbor, and myself, not as three separate entities but as three dimensions of one Mystery. To abide by the essence of the law requires that we live and relate to everyone "with all [our] heart, with all [our] soul, with all [our] mind, and with all [our] strength" (Mark 12:29). We often keep the letter of the law but nonetheless miss the point of it, because morality has to do with vitality—that is, with giving our all to all. Obedience to the letter of the law without embracing its spirit does nothing to

enhance the bond of love with God/neighbor/self that is the true
purpose of your commandments.

If your law is written upon our hearts, if the summons to love is
built into our being, then morality is truly an imperative. I must
do what love demands, not in order to avoid punishment when
this life ends, but in order to avoid a kind of death this side of
the grave. I would die physically if I failed to comply with the
imperative to breathe. I die spiritually when I do not comply
with the dictates of love. Surely the world would be a different
place if everyone were attentive and responsive to the voice of
love within. Because I am not always attuned to that voice, I
must ask, What prevents me from hearing it? What keeps me
from responding to it? Morality requires self-knowledge and the
willingness to work against those forces that stifle the innate
impulse that moves me to do good.

In the quest to live upstanding, moral lives, it is easy to fall prey
to the temptation to root out what seems inconsistent with good-
ness. It is difficult to resist this instinct, especially because it is
motivated by the desire to become a better person. But like the
landowner who instructs his servant to let the weeds and wheat
grow together (Matt. 13:24), we do well to abide our imperfec-
tion. This approach to morality is humbling, because we are
faced with a mercy not dependent upon our efforts, our having
made ourselves worthwhile. We can live with our "darkness" if
we have been blessed by your light. We can abide our faults if
we allow ourselves to rest in your mercy that embraces us at our
best and at our worst.

❧ *Personal Reflections* ❦

Chapter 13

Sin

What is actual sin? Actual sin is any willful thought, desire, word, action, or omission forbidden by the law of God.

A CATECHISM OF CHRISTIAN DOCTRINE

Sin occurs when self-image and personal willfulness become so important that one forgets, represses, or denies one's true nature, one's absolute connectedness and grounding in the divine power that creates and sustains the cosmos.

GERALD MAY, *WILL AND SPIRIT*

Sin, according to the Bible, followed close on the heels of creation. The story of Adam and Eve's fall from innocence is meant to convey the reality of the human condition: we live apart from the bliss of our origins. Where life was once a flow, it is now a struggle. Where we once existed in unselfconscious union with God and with all creation, we are now burdened with the awareness of our differences and live in a state of competition—survival of the fittest—as Marcus Borg claims:

Within the Christian tradition "the fall" has commonly been understood to mean "the fall *into sin.*" It has also been associated with the notion of "original sin," which is not simply the *first* sin, but a sinfulness that is transmitted to every individual in every generation. Clearly the Hebrew storyteller is saying that something has gone wrong. Life began in paradise but is now lived outside the garden, in an exile of hard labor, suffering, pain, violence, and fragmentation.[1]

This state of affairs is the consequence of what the church calls "original sin." I was taught, as I shared earlier, that every human being came into the world with a soul marked with this sin. The waters of Baptism were required to purge it, but even after that cleansing its effects remained for a lifetime. I now know that although I am made in the image and likeness of God, I am prone to that which runs counter to God. Certainly, then, there is truth in the notion that the sour soil of my conflicted self gives rise to the thoughts and behaviors we call sins. However, prior to the conflicted self there is the self at one with God. In other words, before there was original sin, there was original holiness.

A sin, as I learned it, was an offense against God. It could be an action or a failure to act; it could be a thought or a feeling. Sin could be major (mortal) or your basic garden variety (venial). It could be intentional—a necessary characteristic of mortal sin—or inadvertent. No matter what the type or degree of sin, the effect was basically the same, however—namely, a damaged relationship with God (a complete break in that relationship in the case of serious sin, or a strain in that relationship for sin of lesser gravity).

Even more weighty than the particulars of sin and its consequence in relation to God was the self-consciousness it engendered. Too much stress on the seriousness of sin and the likelihood that I could fall prey to it produced a burdensome self-awareness—scrupulosity in its most serious form. The fight against sin called for vigilance, along with a stance of readiness to resist even the "near occasion" of sin. For a person caught in this sin-consciousness, life became a matter of wearisome warfare against the forces and sources of sin—including one's self.

Because I was guilty of sin, I spent a good deal of time and energy in an attitude of repentance. In my case, this amounted to self-castigation, promises to reform, and meager attempts to make up for my wrongdoings. None of these efforts seemed to stem the tide that carried me quickly back to the familiar shores of sin, and to the all-too-familiar confines of the confessional. I recall celebrating my thirteenth birthday with a trip to confession. As I stood outside the church reflecting on the dark state of my soul, I had the thought, "How can someone so young be so messed up?" Now, even though I am less obsessed with sin, I sometimes wonder how someone so old can still be in that state! My imperfect self reminds me of the wise statement I once saw on the back of a small packet of sugar: "Experience helps us recognize our mistakes when we make them again."

Confession, as the Sacrament of Reconciliation was once called, was the means the Catholic Church made available for the forgiveness of sins. By confessing your sins to a priest, including the number of times you committed them—offering the proverbial "grocery list"—you could wipe the slate clean, get a fresh start, and experience the relief of knowing that you were back in God's good graces. Everyone who grew up in a religious denomination that offered confession has memories and stories about this often traumatic experience. In the first of a trilogy of books about his upbringing, motivational speaker John Powers humorously describes a fictionalized account of his first confession:

> As I mentally reviewed the classroom mock confessions . . . I could hear Depki who was standing in line behind me mumbling to himself. Man he was talking double figures.
>
> My mind started rattling off a lot of Our Fathers and Hail Mary's while constantly interspersing between them the left-hand fingers, disobeying my parents, and right-hand fingers, lying. Mumbling came from the other side of the window. The confession of the kid from the other side. I silently started praying faster to get my mind off the mumbling. We had been warned that we'd burn plenty for listening to someone else's confession.
>
> . . . I heard the wooden panel slide back from my window. This was it. "Bless me Father, for I have sinned . . ."
>
> He went on and on. First confession and I had to have the luck of drawing a dedicated priest. . . . What were those kids who were waiting in line outside the door thinking? Helger's probably mumbling to Depki "Christ, that Ryan must've done some beauts."[2]

This exaggerated account of confession illustrates the experience I remember from my youth. I spent many long hours shamefully naming and claiming my sinfulness. And as in the confession described above, I did so with an awkward fear of what others, the priest included, might think of me.

Since that time I have spent many long hours on the other side of the "wooden panel," listening to the often sincere, and sometimes neurotic, declaration of penitents longing to be cleansed of their sin. The accumulated experience of being a confessor has left me with the conviction that most of us are better than we think, and that we would do well to count our blessings along with our sins.

Sin is not only one of the most fearsome words in our religious vocabulary; it is also one of the most important. Sin names a truth that must not be denied and that is expressed well by St. Paul when he states, "Instead of doing the good things I want to do, I carry out the sinful things I do not want" (Rom. 7:19). I am not able to consistently function in a manner that is in keeping with my best self, and I am often my own worst enemy. Awareness of our sinfulness is necessary knowledge. The sense of compunction that that knowledge engenders can, if I don't turn against myself, help turn me to God. The humbling awareness of my inability to live as I ought has helped me to recognize and embrace a new understanding of sin. And the experience of confession, despite its negative tone, has taught me that forgiveness is a concrete reality.

Sin is a very real phenomenon, but it need not divert our focus from God, nor does it necessarily create self-negativity. From a spiritual perspective, sin is more than actions, thoughts, and so on; it is a dimension of our very self, our "shadow." We are in sin even when we are at our best, because sin has to do with the fact that we are not yet a finished product, and with the truth that our incompleteness causes us to be alienated from, blind to, and ignorant of the union with God that is at the heart of who we are. Sin, in other words, is a way of being in the world that is out of touch with the truth of God's oneness with us in our brokenness. Dick Westley speaks to this understanding of sin:

> The sin that Jesus fought to overcome is . . . alienation, division, and fragmentation in humankind and in our world. . . . Since sin is now viewed as a state as well as an act, it is no longer enough for us to see to it that we don't "commit" sins, we now must be careful to examine our lives to see whether we aren't actually "living in" sin.[3]

Because I have come to realize that the state of sin in which I live cannot be overcome, I have been challenged to embrace a new understanding of repentance. I now recognize that repentance refers less to my attempts to change my ways, and more to my attitude about God, whose loving and merciful presence enfolds me unconditionally.

Sufis—Muslim mystics—ask a question that makes sense to me: "Is repentance always being aware of our sin, or never being aware of our sin?" I used to believe that the more aware of my sins I was, the less likely I would be to commit them again. "Never being aware of our sin" is not a denial of the reality of our wrongdoing, but a choice to focus on God's undefeated mercy. This is true repentance (change), for it shifts my gaze from my imperfect self to my sacred Self, the presence of God within and beneath my folly.

Most of the thoughts and actions we were taught were sins are better understood as symptoms, indications of the deeper dis-ease of our blindness to, and ignorance of, God's indwelling. But if we mature spiritually, we are less distracted by the knowledge of our sins or the presence of their symptoms, for we know that we continue to abide in God even in the midst of intentional sin. Though we may be unaware of it most of the time, there remains a dimension of us that is intimate with God no matter what, as St. Paul affirmed: "For I am certain of this; neither death nor life, no angel, no prince, nothing that exists, nothing still to come, not any power, or height or depth, nor any created thing, can ever come between us and the love of God" (Rom. 8:38–39). This is a truly radical statement that, if we took it to heart, could help us counter the too-prevalent tendency toward self-loathing that is fostered by many well-meaning religious authorities.

Those charged with my early religious formation did a good job of instilling in me a fear of the "fires of hell"—a fear that no longer dominates my consciousness. I now realize that, in the words of author Anne Lamott, "We are not punished for the sin, but by the sin."[4] When I do not live in a manner that is consonant with my God-self, I experience a bit of hell on earth. I know firsthand the inner unrest that dispels peace, the at-oddsness with myself that makes it difficult to be silent and alone. The punishment that sin inflicts has its day here and now; its pain is not the vengeful doing of an angry God, but the self-inflicted effect of my disharmony, my failure to be at one with myself. The turmoil that is "punishment by the sin" is also an invitation to be reconciled within. This, I now realize, is accomplished not by "coming clean" in the confessional, although that encounter can help us achieve inner peace, but by being open to the truth of God's merciful indwelling and being willing to live in sync with what that presence calls us to—namely, compassion for ourselves and for all others.

The Sacrament of Reconciliation is not an encounter where forgiveness is imparted, but an event where the ongoing mercy of God is celebrated. Some years ago I received a phone call from a student who wanted to make an appointment for confession. When she arrived the next day she said: "I'm not sure why I'm here. I mean, why do I have to go through the operator when I can dial direct?" The best response I know to that question was penned by Robert Farrar Capon when he said, in response to a similar question, "Why go to a party when you can drink by yourself?"[5] The Sacrament of Reconciliation is a communal affair, even though it is generally a "party of two." The priest is a representative of the church, the community that our sinfulness affects. When we are not our best selves, our brokenness diminishes the whole.

Many people find that confessing their condition of sin and its consequent behaviors to a friend, or to the person they offended, to be a more meaningful form of reconciliation with God than a formal, sacramental confession. Others, because they continue to value participation in the sacramental life of the church, prefer to "go through the operator." In either case, or in both, what is important is to acknowledge the reality of sin and its effects, and to move beyond the self-focus that is often a consequence of sin.

I wouldn't hesitate to wager that all of the great saints and mystics had a clear sense that they were sinful. But beyond this, my guess is that they knew they were *forgiven* sinners. This awareness, and the humility it gives birth to, roots us in the womb of God's life-giving mercy. Our sin is forgiven; we are known in our lostness. Our inner fragmentation is held together; we are one with the One in whose mercy we are bathed. We live in a union with God that not even sin can destroy.

I know all too well that I am capable of sins of commission and omission. I do what I ought not, and I fail to do what I should. But preoccupation with sins of this sort no longer consumes me. Instead, I am aware of the condition of sin that is the blind and ignorant out-of-sync-with-God way in which I often go about my life, a way of living that is evident when I overreact to my ineptness rather than humbly accepting myself as lovable despite it. It is also visible, at least to me, when I go at life in too forceful a manner, trying to make things happen when and as I wish, rather than going with the flow of life's sacred unfolding even when it doesn't feel very sacred. This alienation from my God-self is my sin, the source of the symptoms that used to distract me. It is this alienation that I must gently but firmly address in order to be healed and at peace.

Meditations

Awareness of and contrition for my sins can be essential for change, or they can keep me mired in self-loathing. My wrongdoing is a felix culpa, a happy fault, for it is an occasion for your mercy. To never be aware of my sin is to always be convinced that I am forgiven, that I continue to live in Love's merciful embrace no matter what. Better to sin and become aware of your unconditional love than to be sinless and live in the illusion that my supposed virtue is the reason I am loved.

I live in sin when ignorance of your indwelling results in identification with my false self. In this case, I am what I do and what others think of me. The source of my worth is my accomplishments and the praise I receive for being successful by human standards. I am free to choose this way of living, but I am not free in it, because to so choose is to be sin's prisoner. My true self, though still "in Love," is shackled by my compromises and lies buried beneath the weight of my attachments. To be reconciled with you, O God, is to know, and to live in sync with, the truth that my worth is based not on my possessions or accomplishments, but on being one who, despite my sin, is the apple of your eye.

The attempt to uproot sin from my life is a mistake—at least as an initial reaction. I must first love myself as one who is sinful. This becomes possible if I accept your love for me as I am. Your forgiveness, which is extended not just when I repent, but even in the state of my lostness, can motivate me to love myself and to be compassionate with the imperfections of others. Everyone *is a forgiven sinner. To embrace this is to be in right relationship with you, my neighbor, and myself. It also frees me from preoccupation with my faults and enables me to enter solitude without fear and relationships without looking for the "splinter" in another's eye.*

Sin is sometimes referred to as "missing the mark." To say that we are sinners is not to say that we are bad people, but that we are people with bad aim! Instead of seeing you in the crosshairs of the eyes of faith, we see only what our physical eyes behold: we see the surface but not the sacred center of creation. Because we fail to see your divinity within ourselves and others, we both act and react in ways that are less than holy. We sin; we miss the mark; we fall short of being who we can be and could be if our vision were better—who we in fact can be if we refocus.

Personal Reflections

Chapter 14

Grace/Salvation

What is grace? Grace is a supernatural gift of God bestowed on us through the merits of Jesus Christ for our salvation.

A CATECHISM OF CHRISTIAN DOCTRINE

I thought when I was young . . . salvation concerned "where will you spend eternity?" . . . But it now seems clear to me that salvation centrally concerns our life in this world.

MARCUS BORG, *THE GOD WE NEVER KNEW*

My childhood notion of grace was that it was a commodity I earned by receiving the sacraments, praying, and keeping the commandments and other rules of behavior. Grace flowed into me like gas into a car; I went to church to "fill 'er up."

There were two kinds of grace: sanctifying (like premium gas) and actual (regular). The former was obtained primarily by receiving the sacraments; it conferred a share in God's life. Sanctifying grace was considered necessary for salvation because, according to the portion of the Catechism quoted in the epigraph above, "it is a supernatural gift." It bestowed supernatural powers—namely, the seven gifts of the Holy Ghost and the three theological virtues referred to in Chapters 4 and 7. To be in the state of sanctifying grace was to be at one's holy best. You could get a lot of miles per gallon with sanctifying grace: it took you a long way down the road to heaven because it brought heaven closer to home.

Actual grace was another matter. It was thought to be a help, a kind of "wind beneath your wings" or a supernatural pat on the back. It was considered necessary because, in the words of the Catechism, "without it we cannot long resist the power of temptation or perform other actions which merit a reward in Heaven."[1] With the help of actual grace, one could see the difference between right and wrong more clearly and have the strength to resist evil and do good. Actual grace enhanced one's ability to run on all cylinders.

A phrase I remember hearing a lot in my youth is "There but for the grace of God go I." I got the impression from this statement that life was a pretty iffy affair, and that the only reason my lot in it happened to be better than somebody else's had to do with God's deciding, arbitrarily, to spare me—this time—and to zap someone else. But for the grace of God I could have been living on the street, I could have been the one injured in an accident, my mother could have thrown out my baseball cards when my parents moved from the house I grew up in. The grace of God was what saved me from disasters large and small.

The notion of grace I learned about was the opposite of *dis*grace. Like Mary, who is hailed as "full of grace," grace-filled people, I thought, sailed through life's trials and tribulations with the flawless finesse of a ballet dancer. Life might not spare them hard times, but you'd never know it by looking at them; they seemed nonplussed, never even tempted to question God when they ended up on the "Job-end" of life's unfair occurrences. Although this is a limited understanding of grace, it is one that has a powerful impact on those who witness it.

I have been privileged to see this sort of gracefulness at work in a young man named Ed, who as I write is eighteen years old and about five weeks into his new life as a quadriplegic. Ed was injured when he slipped on some rocks while fishing. The irreparable damage to his spinal cord has changed forever his physical mobility, but it hasn't damaged his spirit. His smile, gentle manner, and positive outlook have won the hearts of the nursing staff and rehabilitation therapists who are working with him. You can tell by looking at Ed that he isn't looking back. Instead, he's learning how to gracefully maneuver his new electric wheelchair.

As the Catechism definition states, grace is given "for our salvation." Within the faith-tradition I grew up in, *salvation* referred to the saving of one's soul, one's abiding with God for all eternity. It was my job, the church told me, to do everything I could to secure entrance into heaven when this life was over. I was to do good, avoid evil, and thus remain in the state of grace; this is what made me eligible for salvation.

There was another requirement for salvation that I stumbled onto merely because I was born and baptized into the Catholic Church. It was a well-known fact among Catholics that there was *extra ecclesiam nulla salus*—that is, no salvation outside Catholicism. Technically speaking, this meant that those who through their own fault did not know that the Catholic Church was the true Church or, knowing it, refused to join it, could not be saved. I always had trouble believing that my non-Catholic friends would end up in hell, but I took consolation in knowing that I had a head start in going north when I died!

Salvation, I was taught, had been won for me by Jesus' death on the cross, but that didn't let me off the hook. Yes, I was saved by the "blood of the Lamb," but my efforts, aided by grace, were required if eternal life was to be mine. The notion that one could be saved merely by faith, by opening to the grace of God's saving act (the sacrifice of Jesus' life) is a Lutheran teaching and, therefore, not open for consideration by Catholics.

Whether achieved by grace, faith, good works, or some combination of them all, salvation was considered an "every person for him/herself" affair. On Judgment Day everyone would stand utterly alone before God and hear, one at a time, the good or bad news that would comprise that person's eternal destiny. Where we were to end up depended a lot on how we treated others, but my impression was that both salvation and damnation were earned by our individual deeds or misdeeds.

When I was young, I didn't know how uncontainable grace was, how utterly beyond my ability it was to earn. But I did become convinced, at a deep level, that I could tap into a source of strength and life that could make me more resemble my best self. Likewise, I didn't know that salvation was about more than me and more than the whereabouts of my soul after my death. But I did gain a sense that how I live now is not unrelated to whatever life beyond this life is about. What I now believe is that both grace and salvation refer to dimensions of reality that are a vital piece of everyday living.

Grace is not a commodity one earns by fulfilling religious requirements; it is not an "it" of any sort. Rather, grace is a word that connotes the truth of our status in God. I am in agreement with Marcus Borg, who indicates that grace has to do with our being fully embraced by the Mystery that is our source and sustenance:

> "You are accepted." This is one of the central meanings of grace. . . . God accepts us just as we are. No "if" statement follows, despite our tendency to add one or more: we are accepted *if* we truly repent, *if* we truly believe. . . . "You are accepted," period, full stop.[2]

Grace is good news to those of us who think and/or feel that we are on the outs with God. It is often surprising, and always humbling.

Grace, as the song says, is also amazing. It surely was for John Newton, the man who authored the words that became the song "Amazing Grace." Newton was a slave-ship captain turned minister. He was a man who was spiritually lost but then found; he was blind and then began to see. For him and for us, grace is gratuitous. But if, like Newton, we are lost and blind, it is not because we lack grace, but because we are not attuned to God's grace-presence. Our own life, and indeed life itself, is the stage upon which the performance of grace never ceases to be enacted.

We do not earn grace; it is a gift given from the start. We are conceived and born in grace. Quickly—due in part to the fact that we all experience love as conditional, dependent on our pleasing those who grant it—we lose a sense for the pervasive presence of grace. But the reality of it is undefeated, and our periodic awakenings to this truth are indeed "graced moments," for they help us see and sense the sacred nature of life and of ourselves.

The birth of a child and the death of one ready to die are graced moments that serve as bookends to life's many (and more subtle) experiences of grace. The rising and setting of the sun are the opening and closing acts of a day that is a play filled with scenes, both joyful and sorrowful, replete with God's surprisingly predictable and unconditional grace.

The danger in this, as in anything given without strings attached, is that we can take it for granted. How often, for instance, have we taken a breath without realizing that every breath we've ever taken has been given to us? How many times have we looked into the eyes of another, whether of a loved one or a stranger, and failed to see the boundless Mystery that every person is a manifestation of? Rather than tapping into the deep well of God's constant, affirming grace-presence as an enabling force, we tend to live a less-than-full life content with what Dietrich Bonhoeffer called "cheap grace." With this attitude grace becomes an excuse, a way to rationalize the continuance of our inauthenticity. Cheap grace, as the term implies, gives us an inferior product, an imitation of the real thing, that can make us feel good, but that has little substance. In my opinion, when the leader of a country calls upon God to bless the decision to wage a preemptive war, he is asking for the cheap grace that will assuage his conscience, and that of his nation, so that what is unjust may appear justified. True grace, on the other hand, challenges us to recognize the full impact of our decisions and actions, and to relate to ourselves and others in a way that leads us, individually and collectively, to a holy wholeness.

Grace, I have discovered, comes wrapped in unlikely packages that we're not inclined to receive gracefully. We often go kicking and screaming down the paths on which life leads us. We are sometimes resentful that our marriages are not easier, that our careers move from peak to valley, and that our health goes south at too early an age. And yet, these very situations are full of grace, because they call us to dig deep and to discover within ourselves what can enable us to embrace life as it is. Anne Lamott writes about "ungraceful grace":

> I don't know why life isn't constructed to be seamless and safe, why we make such glaring mistakes, things fall so short of our expectations, and our hearts get broken and our kids do scary things, and our parents get old and don't always remember to put pants on before they go out for a stroll. I don't know why it's not more like it is in the movies, why things don't come out neatly and lessons can't be learned when you're in the mood for learning them, why love and grace often come in such motley packaging.[3]

Perhaps grace is not so graceful after all. Perhaps it's in our *dis*graced moments that the mystery of God's presence can impact us most. When we glimpse Divinity in the dust or, better put, when we see the Divinity *of* dust and pain and all things and all people unattractive to us, then we've met grace face to face and can be led beyond our blindness to an acceptance of reality as it is, and of God, who is never apart from it.

Many of us meet "disguised grace" in relationships with those we find it difficult to be with. This happens in marriage, in family, in religious life, at work, and wherever people come together. But there is grace here if we are open to growth, because it is the person we least want to be with who has the most to teach us about ourselves. For what we dislike about another is often a projection of aspects of ourselves that we don't like or that we judge to be character flaws, personality quirks, physical defects, and the like.

One of the many times I've experienced this occurred in a church setting where a woman who considered herself an expert in liturgy performed her assigned task of reading in a way that struck me, and many others, as overly pious. It took every ounce of restraint I could muster to keep from leaping out of my presider's chair to escort her from the sanctuary. When I discussed my reaction with my spiritual director, Rose, she wisely pointed out how like that woman I am. After resisting my impulse to escort Rose from the room, I realized the truth of her insight. It was not that I too was overly pious, but that I, in my relaxed manner of conducting liturgy, was as attached to the rightness of my style as this woman was to hers. What irked me was not so much her manner of reading as her cocky sureness that her way was the right way.

When I see that what I see in others is in me, and when I begin to accept the me I see in them, I can be less critical and more at ease with those who upset me. It was this kind of dynamic that Jesus alluded to when he spoke about taking the log out of our own eye before removing the splinter from another's eye (Matt. 7:3).

Anne Lamott says, "I do not understand the mystery of grace—only that it meets us where we are but does not leave us where it found us."[4] This understanding of grace as transformative dovetails with the idea of salvation as a present reality. Salvation is not only about life beyond this life, but also about the quality of life *this* side of the grave.

Most of us walk this earth not always, or even usually, at

full strength. We have broken hearts, wounded spirits, weakened bodies. We stand in need of healing and consolation at the same time that we are called to give them. Salvation refers to the effect that grace can have on us. The word *salvation* derives from the same Latin source as the word *salve*. A salve is an ointment used to sooth and to heal, or the act of applying such a balm. In the midst of our flawed humanness, we are salved and saved. This is accomplished not by Jesus' having atoned for our sins by his suffering and death, but by what he, for Christians, is a sign of—the fact that Divinity accompanies humanity. We are never apart from God, no matter how dire the circumstances. We are, even now, "seated at God's right hand." We may never be cured of our wounds, but we can be healed (made whole of soul) by the soothing awareness and power of God's abiding presence.

Salvation is a reality here and now. It is a personal/individual phenomenon, but it is also communal. No person is an island apart from the whole. For better and for worse we sail in the same ship; and together, not apart, we live in the grace-filled and saving presence of God.

Insofar as salvation implies that a dimension of heaven is here, it is our interactions with one another that make the experience of salvation a reality. It is when we give as well as receive, when we care as well as allow others to care for us, that we participate in the salvation of God's being in our midst. A story with Chinese origins illustrates this truth. A person died and was transported to hell. The scene there was of a large banquet with abundant amounts of delicious food. The hell of it was that the chopsticks that the inhabitants used to feed themselves were so long that people weren't able to get the food to their mouths. In a split second the deceased was taken to heaven. He was amazed to see the exact same scene there, complete with supersized chopsticks; the difference was that each banquet guest in heaven ate his/her fill because they all fed each other.

We are the means through which God's soothing ointment is applied. In moving beyond the concern of satisfying our own needs, we become instruments of salvation, sacraments of God's healing and nurturing presence for a wounded world.

When a person embraces a spiritual understanding of God, life, and religion, the notion of a Judgment Day becomes less ominous and more immediate. The divine judgment is seen not as a moment at the end of life when we are "sentenced" to our eternal reward or punishment, but as an ongoing reality, a point Flannery O'Connor makes in her short story "You Can't Be Any Poorer Than Dead":

As for Judgment Day . . . every day is Judgment Day. . . . Ain't you old enough to have learnt that yet for yourself? Don't everything you do, everything you have ever done, work itself out right or wrong before your eye and usually before the sun is set?[5]

It is a kind of Judgment Day when, despite our intention to remain anonymous, our furtive act of generosity is rightly attributed to us. Likewise, judgment is meted out when our lies of word or deed come to light and our guilt is revealed. Everyday judgment days are not about eternal commendation or condemnation as much as they are confrontations and invitations to live in a way that is consonant with the reality of God's indwelling today.

I used to think that grace was a commodity that made it possible for me to acquire salvation. If I stored up enough of

it I was assured of an eternity of bliss. Because my understanding of things religious is now more incarnate, I have
come to view grace not as quantitative, but as relational—a
quality of presence, the "Godness" that informs my being.
The notion of salvation that I once thought referred exclusively to the condition of my soul in the afterlife I now realize is also about the freedom and wholeness with which I
live here and now, and which I mediate to others when I am
open to grace.

Meditations

Grace is not something we have more or less of; it is a concept that refers to the truth that we have all of you we need. We are graced people not because we are blessed with health, intelligence, talent, and the like, but because we are gifted with the life of your Spirit. Grace is the divine presence, power, and passion incarnate within us that enable us to live dynamic lives, and to meet life in its good times and bad with the fullness of your grace.

It is tempting to think that grace abounds in us only when we are at our best, when we are able to deal with life gracefully, when, for instance, we are strong in the face of loss or at peace in the midst of turmoil. But grace is a constant. In the midst of tears and fears, you are one with us. When we are lost and lonely, we may be out of touch with grace, but the reality of it permeates us nonetheless. It is difficult to be still and to know you when all is dark, but to do so usually brings a sense of light and peace. But should we remain in the dark spiritually/emotionally, faith can still affirm that the darkness is graced with your divinity

Grace is a blessing and a curse. The former is obvious enough, given that grace has to do with the experience of your presence and the empowerment that comes with it. But grace can also be

experienced as a burden. When we are challenged, whether by others or by your indwelling Spirit, to live with integrity and authenticity, this too is grace—the opposite of "cheap grace." It is your summons to be our true selves—a process that can be very uncomfortable. But it is your summons, and therefore, a matter of grace.

Salvation is primarily about experiencing your reign, O God, here and now. It is not, therefore, something we earn, but a reality we awake to. When we see and enter into the sacred present, we taste heaven. When we savor our relationship with people and with the earth as a dimension of your divinity, we glimpse the bliss to which we are eternally called. When we realize that our very self is an epiphany, albeit an imperfect one, of your presence, we can walk in the freedom, peace, and joy that characterize your kingdom.

The salvation we experience this side of death is not a resting-place. Although it is comforting to realize that we live in your embrace, that same awareness moves us to bring the salve of your healing to others. To be saved is to enter into the saving action of your Spirit. Those who know with their hearts that salvation is a reality for them feel your divine dis-ease that draws them out of themselves and into the world. Salvation is the foundation for discipleship.

𝕊 *Personal Reflections* 𝕊

Chapter 15

Heaven / Hell / Purgatory

What are the rewards or punishments appointed for
men after the particular judgment? The rewards or
punishments appointed for men after the particular
judgment are heaven, purgatory, or hell.
A CATECHISM OF CHRISTIAN DOCTRINE

Heaven is not a reward that gets added on to a life of
faith, hope, and love, but it is simply the end of that
life . . . the working out of the life that is oriented by
these principles. . . . Hell is not some external place
of arbitrary punishment that gets assigned for sin,
but simply the working out of sin itself. . . . [P]urga-
tory belongs to present experience. . . . [T]he kind of
"suffering" envisaged in purgatory is not an external
penalty that has to be paid, but is . . . the painful
surrender of the ego-centered self.
JOHN MACQUARRIE, PRINCIPLES OF CHRISTIAN THEOLOGY

Taken literally, which was the only way to take religious concepts when I was young, heaven, hell, and purgatory were considered places. The former was a place of bliss peopled by angels and those who believed in God, and in Jesus as God's only Son. Also present were the good people who put their faith into practice and who died in the state of grace. Heaven was a place of rest, of peace, and of happiness. It was where you could lounge around and do forever all the things you enjoyed most on earth without the consequences. In heaven you could eat all the pizza and hot-fudge sundaes you wanted and never gain weight!

I heard a lot of talk about some people having a higher place in heaven, a seat or cushion close to the throne. This area was reserved for the saints, for priests and nuns, and maybe for Billy Graham. People who suffered a lot were also thought to have a higher place—those who lived with chronic pain, for instance, and probably everyone who lived in India (even though most of them were Hindu; their suffering, I presumed, made up for their not being Christian).

I was told by someone that in heaven everyone would be thirty-three years old, the age at which Jesus died, give or take a few. I never got confirmation on that, and was perplexed as to how that could happen, especially for those who died before having reached that age. In any case, I find that the older I get the better this theory sounds!

Hell was heaven's opposite. Heaven was up; hell was down. Heaven was bliss; hell was torment. Heaven was God's abode; hell was the venue of the devil (a.k.a. Satan). Satan was a fallen angel whose job it was to tempt us so that we would sin and, thereby, miss the bliss. It took only one mortal sin on your soul at death to land you in the flames of hell forever, as *A Catechism of Christian Doctrine* states: "Those are punished in hell who die in mortal sin; they are deprived of the vision of God and suffer dreadful torments, especially that of fire, for all eternity."[1]

As indicated above, the pain of hell was depicted as physical, but it also had an emotional/spiritual element. This would consist, for those of us condemned to endure it, of the awareness that we were not, and never would be, where we were meant to be: at one with God. Like an unfaithful lover separated from the beloved, we would be plagued for eternity by the heartache of realizing that we were responsible for our distance from the Divine.

Purgatory was situated between heaven and hell. Unlike the other two, it was a temporary abode, a place of suffering in which we would remain until the price for our sins had been paid. Once purged of the effects of sin we would become worthy of heaven, eligible to join the ranks of the saved. We could get time off from purgatory while still on earth by gaining indulgences and by "offering up" our temporal suffering; and we could get others' souls out of purgatory by praying for them.

Though I never heard it spoken of this way, I tended to think of purgatory as having an anteroom, a small addition called limbo, which housed those babies—and some others, I supposed—who died without being baptized. Limbo was neither bliss nor torment. It was, like vanilla ice-cream, not bad, but it lacked oomph!

I never questioned the geographical reality of heaven, hell, or purgatory; they were as real to me as the earth on which I walked. I took their existence as a literal fact and lived in hope of heaven and fear of hell and purgatory throughout my youth. Although I no longer believe what I was taught, those teachings helped me realize that some sort of life continues after the death of our bodies, and that how we conduct ourselves now is not unrelated to what we may experience later.

At this point in my life I am not as interested in getting to heaven as I am in being there! To speak of heaven (as well as hell and purgatory/limbo) is not to designate a geographical place apart from where we are now. Heaven refers to a quality of life that envelops us in the present, as theologian Gregory Baum states: "We are summoned to be open to God's Word, to become listeners, to remain learners, to continue growing. . . . This is heaven."[2] Heaven is where God is, and the God I have come to embrace is omnipresent, as is the divine invitation to become fully alive here as well as there, now as well as later, within as well as beyond this life. We live in the presence of the Holy twenty-four/seven.

Though it is not possible, this side of the grave, to constantly experience the bliss that is life in God, I live in the conviction that every breath and heartbeat, every wink and blink, every step, and every encounter with another person happens within the enveloping presence of the mystery that is God. This only-sometimes-felt realization enables us to be at peace not only when all is well, but also when all is in turmoil. It makes us capable of going with the flow of life in good times and in bad, for richer and for poorer, in sickness and in health; for Divinity is wedded to humanity, and the ups and downs of our relationship with God take place in the heavenly home that is the temple of our bodies and the cathedral of our earth.

Heaven is here when parents marvel at the premature birth of their child and again, years later, when that same child makes them grandparents. That same couple may sense the sacred as they realize, in their aging and illness, that life is short, and that they have been fortunate to experience its joys and sorrows together. Heaven is not a place of perfection, but the perfection (rightness) of *this* place and of our lives, in all their flawed holiness.

As with heaven, hell is not a place that we believe, or do not believe, exists; rather, it is a reality that can be experienced in life as we know it. Again I turn to Baum for support of this view: "We may close ourselves from the divine Word, we may resist the summons that surrounds us, we may make up our minds never to listen . . . and eventually die in isolation from the dialogue with others which is the source of life. . . . This is hell."[3]

Along with this chosen isolation, the hell that is here may consist of the pain felt in situations that are within our power to prevent: war, poverty, famine, homelessness, abuse, and the like. Those who are victims of natural disasters such as earthquakes, floods, and tornadoes may also experience a kind of hell on earth. Others know the hellishness of personal/emotional pain occasioned by, for instance, the untimely loss of loved ones. And there is the hell we live through when we stubbornly choose to run from the reality of ourselves and our lives in a futile attempt to control our destiny.

We come face to face with this sort of hell when we encounter the self we have lived in denial of, or have projected onto others. Poet David Whyte writes about this truth while commenting on Dante's *Comedia* and, in particular, Dante's desire to circumvent hell:

> Through this gate he will experience all the parts of himself he feels are inferior to his needs, and all the newborn lives he had smothered before they could disturb his stable delusions. In short, the most fearful parts of ourselves that we as human beings hide but must eventually confront.[4]

The hell of our own interior fears, insecurities, and falseness is one that we attempt to avoid by living busy, noisy lives. But by facing the pain that awaits us there, in our murky depths, we can become shamans, compassionate guides capable of accompanying others on their inner journey.

It has been said that religious people believe in hell and spiritual people have been there. The distinction hinted at in this statement is not a judgment affirming the primacy of spirituality over religion, but an acknowledgment of the truth that the Spirit is the guts of religion, and that we can grow in it when we "hit the wall" of our inability to cope with life at its worst. We can become better rather than bitter by facing what afflicts us if we have the awareness that everything that happens is meant to teach us holiness—that is, to make us more humbly aware of our smallness and more gratefully open to God's greatness in us.

I received the message soon after getting to the hospital one Wednesday morning: the wife of a patient on the seventh floor wanted to talk with a priest. Paula, a bright and articulate woman in her mid-forties, had recently moved to Colorado with her husband, who had just had surgery to repair a broken leg. She was in need of support as she tried to make the difficult decision about whether to remain in the state despite her husband's inability to work, or to return to whence they came—an unhappy prospect, since they'd left behind a dysfunctional family situation.

Paula had been through the hell of an abusive childhood and a failed marriage with an alcoholic first husband. Now, just when her life seemed to be on track, this unforeseen event had occurred. They were without a home, job, friends nearby, and money. Fortunately, they were not without faith. As we talked, it became obvious to me that Paula and her husband had entrusted their lives to God. They knew that they would be all right no matter what happened because this situation, like others they had faced, would deepen their relationship with God and with each other. I found it uplifting to be with people who chose to become better through hard times.

One could say that the pain we experience in life is not only our hell, but our purgatory as well. For when our experiences smooth our rough edges, burn away the dross, or refine our character in some way, it is as if we are being readied to abide with God—to be in sync with the holiness at the heart of us.

When Jesus tells his disciples, "[It] is easier for a camel to pass through the eye of a needle than for a rich man to enter the kingdom of heaven" (Matt. 19:24), he is referring not to monetary wealth, but to the "baggage" that is our false self. When we detach from (or die to) what we think/feel makes us worthwhile—appearance, intelligence, accomplishments, and the like—we begin to experience a purgation that can lead to the freedom and joy that comprise the kingdom of God here and now.

Anthropologist Ashley Montague has said that the greatest distance known to humanity spans the difference between who we are called to be, and who we have in fact become. We all fall short of our potential, our vocation to be sacraments of the Divine in our thoughts, words, and actions. But we are all given, through life's challenges (hell), the opportunity to die to the false, ego-centered self (purgatory), and to realize our God-self (heaven).

I used to live my life ruled by the desire to avoid punishments and attain rewards. This was generally true in the give-and-take of my relationships with people, and it was always true in relation to God, whom I considered the one who made the judgment as to whether I would get what I feared or what I desired beyond this life. I am now, thankfully, less concerned about rewards and punishments, and more convinced that I can live this life in a way that makes heaven, hell, and purgatory present realities. I can sense the joy of being at one with the Divine, I can be alienated from that reality, and I can experience the trials that call me to die to what is false so that I can live in the truth, joy, peace, and freedom that are God's kingdom.

Meditations

If heaven is the venue of your omnipresent Spirit, then it cannot be a specific place, for you are a boundless reality. The location of heaven is within; it is the heart and soul of creation. The word heaven *refers to the incomprehensible dimension of life: the bliss of our being, the mystery of this moment, and the perfection of the present. In this heaven, everything and everyone is as it is and ought to be. Spinoza once said that "reality and perfection are one and the same." To see the perfection, the beauty, the rightness that lie beneath the often marred surface of reality is to see heaven. To live at peace with the often chaotic tenor of our life is to experience heaven's hereness.*

To speak of the "hereness" of heaven is to say, figuratively, that we live in your embrace O God. At this very moment, we are, wherever we are, in you, in whom "we live and move and exist" (Acts 17:28). When we cease to imagine you as a person apart from us, whose home is heaven imagined as a place apart from us, every place becomes a place where you can be found. Where we live, where we work, where we shop, where we play, and where we pray are all replete with your divinity. Heaven is not a reward for a life well lived; it is an experience of you, a sense of the sacred alive in our midst.

Hell is not a furnace of flames; it is not a place of punishment. Hell is the experience of suffering that results from alienation. We are living in hell when we live at odds with our true self. When we hold fast to the ego's will and way, we resist and dismiss you, whose Spirit beckons us to surrender, to trust, to "let God be God" in us. When you are God outside of us, our life is hell, because there is a constant sense that we must measure up to something or someone whose love is conditional and who has the power to judge and condemn us.

Hell can be a very personal/individual experience, but it can also be political/social. It can be the result of our own choices, or be imposed by others. It can be limited or catastrophic in its proportions. Evil flourishes not only in the recesses of our hearts, but in our city streets as well. Life is a collective hell when political policy is created that widens the gap between the rich and poor, or when the taking of life is permitted by calling it capital punishment. Hell happens when an appeal to collective fears and national allegiance gives birth to the amassing of military might and the creation of missile defense systems.

Because the term purgatory *refers to "the painful surrender of the ego-centered self" (as Macquarrie said in the chapter's epigraph), we experience its refining fires whenever circumstances require more of us than we would like to give, but we give nonetheless. When we are stretched by a relationship to set aside our preferences for the sake of the other, purgatory is a reality. When, as a result of our refusal to breach confidentiality, we incur the wrath of another, we die to the self that wants to be*

known and loved. We visit purgatory in this life when painful occurrences, whether chosen or imposed, lead us beyond who we are, to become who we are called to be.

⚹ *Personal Reflections* ⚹

A Personal Postscript

The contents of this book trace the change in my understanding of the religious teachings I learned in childhood. The particulars of my religious awakening may differ from yours, but I sense that more and more of us have come to see and to believe ancient truths in new ways. The movement away from traditional interpretations situates us on the perimeter of institutional/organized religion; but the margins, more than mainstream, are a place of hope and vitality. It is from this peripheral place that the status quo is challenged by people whose love for God and longing for spiritual nourishment move them to seek a sense of the sacred both within themselves and beyond their faith tradition. We need not live in opposition to those who continue to find meaning in what they have always believed, but I am convinced that ours is a necessary voice, and that we are a significant witness to them as they are to us. For the truth we all seek is found not in isolation from those who differ from us, but in dialogue with them.

I am certain that the last chapter of my religious/spiritual story is not yet begun – or, if begun, is not complete. For if we are truly open to the dynamism of the Spirit we may come to reject some of what we now believe. We may re-embrace some of what we once held dear. We may come to affirm truths that have yet to present themselves to us. In any case or in all, I hope we remain open to the Spirit whose guidance and wisdom have brought us where we are and will take us where we need to go. It is the Spirit of a mighty Mystery; and a willingness to go with its flow makes for a life full of meaning and surprise wherein we experience the joy that comes with claiming a faith worth believing.

Endnotes

Introduction

1. Joseph Campbell, *Thou Art That*, ed. Eugene Kennedy (Novato, CA: New World Library, 2001), p. xv.
2. Ibid., p. 59.
3. Ibid., p. xvii.
4. William Johnston, ed., *The Cloud of Unknowing* (New York: Image Books, 1973), p. 1.

Chapter 1: Religion

1. Joseph Campbell, *Thou Art That*, ed. Eugene Kennedy (Novato, CA: New World Library, 2001), p. xix.
2. Robert Farrar Capon, *Health, Money, and Love and Why We Don't Enjoy Them* (Grand Rapids, MI: Eerdmans, 1990), p. 30.
3. Carl Woodring and James Shapiro, eds., *The Columbia Anthology of British Poetry* (New York: Columbia Univ. Press, 1995), p. 444.
4. Marcus Borg, *The God We Never Knew* (San Francisco: HarperCollins, 1997), p. 5.
5. Thomas Merton, *Opening the Bible* (Collegeville, MN: The Liturgical Press, 1970), pp. 29-30.

Chapter 2: Father

1. Joseph Campbell, *The Power of Myth* (New York: Doubleday, 1988), p. 49.
2. Michael J. Himes, *Doing the Truth in Love* (Mahwah, NJ: Paulist Press, 1995), p. 19.
3. Marcus Borg, *The God We Never Knew* (San Francisco: Harper-Collins, 1997), p. 12.
4. Annie Dillard, *For the Time Being* (New York: Vintage Books, 1999), p. 177.

Chapter 3: Son

1. Robert Farrar Capon, *Hunting the Divine Fox* (New York: Seabury Press, 1974), p. 90.
2. Marcus Borg, *Jesus: A New Vision* (San Francisco: HarperCollins, 1987), p. 2.
3. James Hillman, *The Soul's Code* (New York: Random House, 1996), p. 189.
4. Carl Woodring and James Shapiro, eds., *The Columbia Anthology of British Poetry* (New York: Columbia Univ. Press, 1995), p. 701.
5. Joseph Campbell, *Thou Art That*, ed. Eugene Kennedy (Novato, CA: New World Library, 2001), p. 19.

Chapter 4: Holy Ghost

1. Michael Morwood, *Is Jesus God?* (New York: Crossroad, 2001), p. 78.

Chapter 5: The Self

1. Etty Hillesum, *An Interrupted Life* (New York: Washington Square Press, 1981), p. 34.
2. Jean Bolen, *The Tao of Psychology* (San Francisco: HarperCollins, 1982), p. 100.

3. Thomas Merton, "The Inner Experience: Notes on Contempl-ation," unpublished manuscript, p. 6.
4. James Finley, *The Awakening Call* (Notre Dame, IN: Ave Maria Press, 1984), p. 95.
5. Edward Galeano, *Walking Words*, trans. Mark Fried (New York: Norton, 1995), p. 151.

Chapter 6: God's Will

1. James Finley, "Meditation in Daily Life" (audio cassette) (Notre Dame, IN: Ave Maria Press, 1982).
2. Robert Farrar Capon, *Hunting the Divine Fox* (New York: Seabury Press, 1974), p. 38.

Chapter 7: Faith

1. Thomas Moore, *Care of the Soul* (New York: HarperCollins, 1992), p. 255.
2. Marcus Borg, *Meeting Jesus Again for the First Time* (San Francisco: HarperCollins, 1994), p. 137.
3. Dick Westley, *A Theology of Presence* (Mystic CT: Twenty-Third Publications, 1988), p. 31.
4. Thomas Merton, *The Seven Storey Mountain* (New York: Harcourt, Brace, 1948), p. 341.
5. Patrick Hart, ed., *Thomas Merton, Monk* (Garden City, NY: Image Books, 1974), p. 170.

Chapter 8: Hope

1. Rick Fields, *Chop Wood Carry Water* (New York: Tarcher/Putnam, 1984), p. 114.
2. Thomas Merton, *The Hidden Ground of Love*, ed. William H. Shannon (New York: Farrar Straus Giroux, 1985), p. 297.
3. David Steindl-Rast, *Gratefulness: The Heart of Prayer* (New York: Paulist Press, 1984), p. 36.

4. T. S. Eliot, *Four Quartets* (New York: Harcourt, Brace & World, 1943), p. 28.
5. Gerald May, *Will and Spirit* (San Francisco: HarperCollins, 1982), p. 310.

Chapter 9: Charity

1. St. Augustine, *The Confessions of St. Augustine*, trans. by F.J. Sheed (New York: Sheed & Ward. 1942), p. 3.
2. Carl Woodring and James Shapiro, eds., *The Columbia Anthology of British Poetry* (New York: Columbia Univ. Press, 1995), p. 136.
3. Robert Farrar Capon, *The Third Peacock* (Minneapolis: Winston Press, 1971), p. 42.
4. Marcus Borg, *Reading the Bible Again for the First Time* (San Francisco: HarperCollins, 2001), p. 301.

Chapter 10: Prayer

1. Stuart Hample and Eric Marshall, *Children's Letters to God* (New York: Workman Publishing, 1991), p. 35.
2. Ibid., p. 37.
3. Ibid., p. 49.
4. *A Catechism of Christian Doctrine*, rev. ed. of *The Baltimore Catechism*, no. 2 (Paterson, NJ: St. Anthony Guild Press, 1954), p. 88.
5. Frederick Buechner, *The Sacred Journey* (San Francisco: Harper-Collins, 1982), pp. 2–3.
6. Robert Farrar Capon, *Health, Money, and Love and Why We Don't Enjoy Them* (Grand Rapid: William B. Eerdmans Publishing Company, 1990), p. 173.

Chapter 11: Sacraments

1. Peter Mayer, "Holy Now."

Chapter 12: Morality

1. Marcus Borg, *Meeting Jesus Again for the First Time* (San Francisco: HarperCollins, 1994), pp. 2–3.

Chapter 13: Sin

1. Marcus Borg, *Reading the Bible Again for the First Time* (San Francisco: HarperCollins, 2001), pp. 77–78.
2. John R. Powers, *The Last Catholic in America* (New York: Popular Library, 1973), pp. 32–33.
3. Dick Westley, *A Theology of Presence* (Mystic, CT: Twenty-Third Publications, 1988), p. 62.
4. Anne Lamott, *Traveling Mercies* (New York: Pantheon Books, 1999), p. 128.
5. Robert Farrar Capon, *Hunting the Divine Fox* (New York: The Seabury Press, 1974), p. 151.

Chapter 14: Grace/Salvation

1. *A Catechism of Christian Doctrine*, rev. ed. of *The Baltimore Catechism*, no. 2 (Paterson, NJ: St. Anthony Guild Press, 1954), p. 21.
2. Marcus Borg, *The God We Never Knew* (San Francisco: HarperCollins, 1997), p. 162.
3. Anne Lamott, *Traveling Mercies: Some Thought on Faith* (New York: Pantheon Books, 1999), pp. 143–144.
4. Anne Lamott, *Traveling Mercies: Some Thought on Faith* (New York: Pantheon Books, 1999), p. 143.
5. Flannery O'Connor, *Flannery O'Connor: The Complete Short Stories* (New York: Farrar, Straus & Giroux, 1979), p. 307.

Chapter 15: Heaven/Hell/Purgatory

1. *A Catechism of Christian Doctrine*, rev. ed. of *The Baltimore Catechism*, no. 2 (Paterson, NJ: St. Anthony Guild Press, 1954), p. 36.

2. Gregory Baum, *Man Becoming* (New York: Herder & Herder, 1971), p. 99.
3. Ibid., pp. 99–100.
4. David Whyte, *The Heart Aroused* (New York: Bantam Double-day Dell, 1994), pp. 282–83.

Bibliography

Augustine of Hippo. *The Confessions of St. Augustine.* Translated by F. J. Sheed. New York: Sheed and Ward, 1942.

Baum, Gregory. *Man Becoming.* New York: Herder & Herder, 1971.

Bolen, Jean. *The Tao of Psychology.* San Francisco: HarperCollins, 1982.

Borg, Marcus. *The God We Never Knew.* San Francisco: Harper-Collins, 1997.

_____. *Jesus: A New Vision.* San Francisco: HarperCollins, 1987.

_____. *Meeting Jesus Again for the First Time.* San Francisco: HarperCollins, 1994.

_____. *Reading the Bible Again for the First Time.* San Francisco: HarperCollins, 2001.

Buechner, Frederick. *The Sacred Journey.* San Francisco: Harper-Collins, 1982.

Campbell, Joseph. *The Inner Reaches of Outer Space.* New York: HarperCollins, 1986.

_____. *The Power of Myth.* New York: Doubleday, 1988.

_____. *Thou Art That.* Edited by Eugene Kennedy. Novato, CA: New World Library, 2001.

Capon, Robert Farrar. *Health, Money, and Love and Why We Don't Enjoy Them.* Grand Rapids, MI: Eerdmans, 1990.

_____. *Hunting the Divine Fox.* New York: Seabury Press, 1974.

_____. *The Third Peacock.* Minneapolis: Winston Press, 1971.

A Catechism of Christian Doctrine. Rev. ed. of *The Baltimore Catechism,* no. 2. Paterson, NJ: St. Anthony Guild Press, 1954.

Coffey, Kathy. *Dancing in the Margins.* New York: Crossroad, 1999.

Dillard, Annie. *For the Time Being.* New York: Vintage Books, 1999.

Eliot, T. S. *Four Quartets*. New York: Harcourt, Brace & World, 1943.

Fields, Rick. *Chop Wood Carry Water*. New York: Tarcher/Putnam, 1984.

Finley, James. *The Awakening Call*. Notre Dame, IN: Ave Maria Press, 1984.

_____. "Meditation in Daily Life" (audio cassette). Notre Dame, IN: Ave Maria Press, 1982.

Galeano, Edward. *Walking Words*. Translated by Mark Fried. New York: Norton, 1995.

Hample, Stuart, and Marshall, Eric. *Children's Letters to God*. New York: Workman Publishing, 1991.

Hart, Patrick, ed. *Thomas Merton, Monk*. Garden City, NY: Image Books, 1974.

Hillesum, Etty. *An Interrupted Life*. New York: Washington Square Press, 1981.

Hillman, James. *The Soul's Code*. New York: Random House, 1996.

Himes, Michael J. *Doing the Truth in Love*. Mahwah, NJ: Paulist Press, 1995.

Johnston, William, ed. *The Cloud of Unknowing*. New York: Image Books, 1973.

Keen, Sam. *Hymns to an Unknown God*. New York: Bantam Books, 1994.

Lamott, Anne. *Traveling Mercies: Some Thoughts on Faith*. New York: Pantheon Books, 1999.

Macquarrie, John. *Principles of Christian Theology*. New York: Scribner, 1966.

May, Gerald. *Will and Spirit*. San Francisco: HarperCollins, 1982.

Merton, Thomas. *The Hidden Ground of Love.* Edited by William H. Shannon. New York: Farrar Straus Giroux, 1985.

_____. "The Inner Experience: Notes on Contemplation." Unpublished manuscript.

_____. *Opening the Bible*. Collegeville, MN: Liturgical Press, 1970.

_____. *The Seven Storey Mountain*. New York: Harcourt, Brace, 1948.

Moore, Thomas. *Care of the Soul*. New York: HarperCollins, 1992.

Morwood, Michael. *Is Jesus God?* New York: Crossroad, 2001.

O'Connor, Flannery. *Flannery O'Connor: The Complete Short Stories*. New York: Farrar, Straus & Giroux, 1979.

Powers, John R. *The Last Catholic in America*. New York: Popular Library, 1973.

St. John of the Cross. *The Collected Works of St. John of the Cross*. Translated by Kieran Kavenaugh and Otilio Rodriguez. Washington, D.C.: Institute of Carmelite Studies Publications, 1973.

Steindl-Rast, David. *Gratefulness: The Heart of Prayer*. New York: Paulist Press, 1984.

Tillich, Paul. *The Courage to Be*. New Haven: Yale Univ. Press, 1952.

Westley, Dick. *A Theology of Presence*. Mystic, CT: Twenty-Third Publications, 1988.

Whyte, David. *The Heart Aroused*. New York: Bantam Doubleday Dell, 1994.

Woodring, Carl, and Shapiro, James, eds. *The Columbia Anthology of British Poetry*. New York: Columbia Univ. Press, 1995.